To dear Helen
Love at Christmas
from Marjie Bryce
2008

Finished reading this delightful
blessed volume June 23.2009.

CHRISTMAS
Miracles

CHRISTMAS
Miracles

True Stories of Joy and Wonder

Edited by Mary Hollingsworth

GUIDEPOSTS
New York, New York

Christmas Miracles
ISBN-13: 978-0-8249-4742-2
Published by Guideposts
16 East 34th Street
New York, New York 10016
www.guideposts.com

Distributed by Ideals Publications, a Guideposts company
2636 Elm Hill Pike, Suite 120
Nashville, Tennessee 37214
Guideposts and Ideals are registered trademarks of Guideposts.

Acknowledgments

Every attempt has been made to credit the sources of copyrighted material used in this book. If any such acknowledgment has been inadvertently omitted or miscredited, receipt of such information would be appreciated.

All material that originally appeared in Guideposts publications is reprinted with permission. Copyright © Guideposts.

Unless otherwise noted, Scripture quotations are from the New Century Version®. Copyright © 1987, 1988, 1991 by Thomas Nelson, Inc. All rights reserved. Quotations designated KJV are from the King James Version of the Bible. Quotations designated NIV are from the Holy Bible, New International Version. Copyright © 1973, 1978, 1984, International Bible Society. Used by permission of Zondervan Bible Publishers. Quotations designated NKJV are from the New King James Version, copyright © 1979, 1980, 1982, Thomas Nelson, Inc., Publishers.

"The Christmas Thief" and "A Cherished Past, A Hopeful Present" published by permission from *Whispers from Heaven*, copyright © 2001, 2002 Publications International, Ltd. "The Bus Riding Angel" taken from *Angel at My Door* by Robert Strand, © 2003 Evergreen Press. (www.evergreenpress.com). Used by permission "Christmas Joy" by Wilma J. Masingale, "God is So Wonderful" by Patti Bierer and "A Teddy Bear Angel" by Katherine Erwin from *When God Sends an Angel* ©2006 Publications International, Ltd. "The Monticello Miracle" by Justin Rodriquez © 13 December 2006. Used by permission of the *Times Herald-Record*, Middletown, NY.

"The Christmas Angels", "Christmas Smiles," and "You are Loved" by Susan Farr Fahncke, "The Blizzard of '82", "Tahira" and "The Watch" by Zarette Beard, "Christmas Miracles" by Connie Wilcox, "The Gift of the Hummingbird" by Marilyn A. Kinsella, "Learning Christmas Love" by Pat J. Sikora, "A Child is Born" by Sue Ferguson, "Jeffrey's Gift" by Donna Lowich, "The New Doll" by Betty R. Graham, "Ordinary People" by Nancy B. Gibbs, "A Christmas to Remember" as told to Greg Asimakoupoulos, "Christmas Tag Miracles" by Mary Hollingsworth, "The Best Christmas Gift" by Joanne K. Hill, "The Christmas Miracle" by Susan Leonard and "A Gift to Each Other" by Kristi Hemingway; are used by permission of the authors.

Editorial, research, and content development managed by Shady Oaks Studio, Bedford, Texas. Team members: Patty Crowley, Rhonda Hogan, Mary Hollingsworth, Mary Kay Knox, Kathryn Murray, Nancy Sullivan, Stephanie Terry, and Barbara Tork.

Library of Congress Cataloging-in-Publication Data
Christmas miracles / edited by Mary Hollingsworth.
    p. cm.
 ISBN 978-0-8249-4742-2
 1. Christmas—Anecdotes. I. Hollingsworth, Mary, 1947–
 BV45.C5765 2008
 242'.335—dc22   2008017539

Cover design by The DesignWorks Group
Photo by The Image Bank
Printed and bound in the United States of America
10 9 8 7 6 5 4 3 2 1

To my sister-in-law and friend,
Kay Shrode—
our family's
special
"Christmas angel"

Contents

Chapter 2: Yuletide Mysteries

Chapter 3: Gifts and Glory

Chapter 4: Christmas Wonder

Chapter 5: Peace and Good Will

Introduction

A journey. A stable. A manger. A Baby. And the Miracle of Christmas was quietly born in a small town some two thousand years ago.

A star. Angels singing. Shepherds watching. Wise men bringing gifts. And the divine birthday party given by God Himself began.

Santa Claus. Glitzy lights. Flashing tree. Shiny packages. And the party once begun still continues, and sometimes in a sadly materialistic modern-day rendition.

Still, as you will see from the wonderful stories in this book, the real miracles of Christmas are still alive and well. People still celebrate the Baby's birth. Still sing the songs of angels. And wise men still follow the star to find Him.

The wonder in the eyes of children is still sparkling. The holy magic that filled that lonely stable so long ago still fills the air of Christmas today. People are kinder.

Friends get together in fun. Families reunite to share their joy. And hope is rekindled every December like the coals of a never-dying fire.

Christmas. It's a miraculous word. A word that brings a smile to your face. A word that exudes warmth and peace and love. Join us now for glimpses of God at work in the lives of His people in celebration of the birth of His precious Son . . . and our Savior.

Christmas miracles are alive and well. And as you turn the pages of this delightful book, you may very well remember how God has touched you at this very special time of year too. Look for Him. Listen for Him. He's always there, lighting the candles on the cake at the party for His Son.

MARY HOLLINGSWORTH

CHAPTER 1

Christmas Angels

An angel of the Lord . . . said, . . . "Don't be afraid . . . Mary . . . will give birth to a son, and you will name him Jesus, because he will save his people from their sins" (Matthew 1:20–21).

$\mathcal{A}$ ngels have always been part of Christmas . . . from the first Christmas until today. They are the glorious beings who announced the miraculous arrival of God's Holy Son on earth in the form of a tiny baby. They are the ones who will blow their trumpets to announce His magnificent return to earth when the time comes. They are God's special messengers. Terrifying. Tender. Defending. Protecting. Watching over us day and night.

The Christmas Angels

SUSAN FARR FAHNCKE

It was December 23. My children and I lived in a teeny, miniature house. Being a single mom, going to college, and supporting my children completely alone, Christmas was looking bleak. I looked around me, realization dawning like a slow, twisting pain. We were poor.

Our tiny house had two bedrooms, both off the living room. They were so small that my baby daughter's crib barely fit into one room, and my son's twin bed and dresser into the other. There was no way they could share a room, so I made my bed every night on the living room floor. The three of us shared the only closet in the house. We were snug, always only a few feet from each other—day and night. With no doors on the children's rooms, I could see and hear them at all times. It made them feel secure and made me feel close to them—a blessing I would not have had in other circumstances.

3

It was late, almost eleven. The snow was falling softly, silently. I was wrapped in a blanket, sitting at the window to watch the powdery flakes flutter in the moonlight, when my front door vibrated with a pounding fist.

Alarmed, I wondered who would be at my home so late on this snowy winter night. I opened the door to find several strangers ginning from ear to ear, their arms laden with boxes and bags.

Confused, but finding their joyous spirit contagious, I grinned right back.

"Are you Susan?" The man stepped forward as he sort of pushed a box at me.

Nodding stupidly, unable to find my voice, I was sure they thought I was mentally deficient.

"These are for you." The woman thrust another box at me with a huge, beaming smile. The porch light and the snow falling behind her cast a glow on her dark hair, lending her an angelic appearance.

I looked down into her box. It was filled to the top with treats, a fat turkey, and all the makings of a traditional Christmas dinner. My eyes filled with tears as the realization of what they were there for washed over me.

Finally coming to my senses, I found my voice and invited them in. Following the husband were two children, staggering with the weight of their packages. The family introduced themselves to me and told me their packages were all gifts for my little family. This wonderful, beautiful family, who were total strangers to me, somehow knew exactly what we needed. They brought wrapped gifts for each of us, a full buffet for me to make on Christmas day, and many "extras" that I could never afford. Visions of a beautiful, "normal" Christmas literally danced in my head. Somehow my secret wish for Christmas was materializing right in front of me. The desperate prayers of a mother alone were heard, and I knew right then that He had sent His angels my way.

My mysterious angels then handed me a white envelope, gave me another round of grins, and each of them hugged me. They wished me a merry Christmas and disappeared into the night as suddenly as they had appeared. What felt like slow-motion time was over in probably less than a couple of minutes.

Amazed and deeply touched, I looked around me at the boxes and gifts strewn at my feet and felt the ache of depression suddenly being transformed into a childlike joy. I began to cry. I cried hard, sobbing tears of the deepest gratitude. A great sense of peace filled me. The knowledge of God's love reaching into my tiny corner of the world enveloped me like a warm quilt. My heart was full. I hit my knees amid all the boxes and offered a heartfelt prayer of thanks.

Getting to my feet, I wrapped myself in my blanket and sat once again to gaze out the window at the gently falling snow. Suddenly I remembered the envelope. Like a child I ripped it open and gasped at what I saw. A shower of bills flitted to the floor. Gathering them up, I began to count the five, ten, and twenty-dollar bills. My vision blurred with tears, I counted the money, then counted it again to make sure I had it right. Sobbing again, I said it out loud. "One hundred dollars."

Even though my "angels" had showered me with gifts, they had somehow understood how desperately money was needed. There was no way they could have known it, but I had just received a disconnect notice from the gas company. I simply didn't have the money needed and feared my family would be without heat by Christmas. The envelope of cash would give us warmth and a tree for Christmas. Suddenly, we had all we needed and more.

I looked at my children sleeping soundly, and through my tears I smiled the first happy, free-of-worry smile in a long, long time. My smile turned into a grin as I thought about tomorrow. Christmas Eve. One visit from complete strangers had magically turned a painful day into a special one that we would always remember. With happiness.

It is now several years since our Christmas angels visited. I have since remarried, and we are happy and richly blessed. Every year since that Christmas in 1993, we choose a family less blessed than we are. We bring them carefully selected gifts, food and treats, and as much money as we can spare. It's our way of passing on what was given to us. It is the "ripple effect" in motion. We hope that the cycle continues and that some day the families that we share with will also pass it on.

Wherever my angels are, I thank you. And so do many other families. Without knowing it, you have touched many lives.

God bless you and all the Christmas angels out there.

The Bus-Riding Angel

ROBERT STRAND

From North Mankato, Minnesota. Two things are always in short supply when you are a college student: sleep and money to go home with. Margarete was away at college, a hard working, diligent college sophomore. She was a resident of a dorm where sleep was a short commodity. Girls being girls, and studies being studies, and boys being subjects of many late-night conversations, the nights seemed pretty short.

The Christmas holidays were soon approaching, which meant a trip home was almost in sight. But as always, college professors haven't much heart and usually schedule tests on the last three or four days preceding vacation. So again, sleep was hard to come by.

Grandma Hendley had sent the funds for Margarete's long bus ride home. As soon as the last class was over, Margarete made her way to the bus depot loaded down with packages and a few presents she had purchased. She quickly purchased her ticket and boarded the bus. She was thankful that her first choice in seats was available—the very last seat next to the back door—where she could stretch out and sleep without interruption all the way to her destination of Mankato, Minnesota.

It felt like such a luxury for her to be able to stretch out with no one to bother her with questions or break into her sleep. The only sounds that filled the bus were those of the other passengers quietly murmuring to each other and the steady humming of the tires on the highway. Such were the comforting, soothing sounds that lulled a tired college sophomore to sleep.

As she slept, the motion of the bus and her tossing pushed her shoulders against the back door. Suddenly, without warning, the back emergency exit door swung open with Margarete wedged against it! Her head and shoulders hung out the open door, awakening her instantly, of course, and she felt herself falling into the blackness of the night towards the hard concrete of the highway. Her first thought was, *I'm going to die!* She frantically grabbed for the door frame to catch herself but missed!

She prayed the most fervent prayer of her short life in just three words: "Jesus, help me!"

And to this day, she says she can almost still feel it—a pair of huge hands caught her and pushed her back into the bus! She quickly looked around, but no one was sitting near enough to her to have touched her!

When the warning light of the open door flashed red, the driver brought the bus to a quick stop and came running down the aisle to check on the problem. Stopping short, he quickly took in the sight of Margarete sitting next to the open door and leaned down to ask her, "Are you all right? I can't understand how it happened. Did you lose anything? Are you afraid? Did you get hurt?" As you can imagine, he was more than a bit upset with the problem.

Still in a sort of shock, Margarete answered, "No sir, no problems."

"Well, then, how did you manage to hold on and not fall out?"

She replied, "I believe I had some heavenly help."

Our Best Customers Ever

MARILYN CALLALY

I leaned against the cooler in the downtown flower shop I ran with my husband, Hugh. Every bit of me ached. Working thirteen hours a day for a week straight has that effect on you, especially when you're coming up on sixty-five years old. But I had to do it. After all, the week leading up to Christmas was one of our busiest.

I glanced at the mirror and laughed. My Santa hat and poinsettia-print shirt were covered with gold and silver glitter. I looked a sight.

Outside, the late December sun cast a glow on the festive decorations. It was about four o'clock in the afternoon on Christmas Eve 1993. The rush was over and our floral designers were gone. The streets were deserted. Even the Salvation Army trio had packed up their instruments and gone home. Nothing to do now but lock the door, clean up the store, and make sure all our holiday orders had been delivered.

Hugh picked up some flower buckets and dumped the water into the sink. "Another holiday down the drain," he said. He'd told the same joke every holiday for the past thirty-five years. Still, I laughed. It was tradition.

Hugh went to straighten up the back room and I grabbed a broom. As I circled the arranger's bench and neared the counter, my eye caught movement outside the front door. Next thing I knew the door flew open and three very large young men walked in. Hugh and I had run this shop for so long we knew everyone in town. Everyone and their guardian angels too. I had no clue who these three were. From the look of them, they were trouble. Grimy black leather jackets and filthy jeans. Wool caps pulled down low. Mean-looking. Real mean. I thought of what Hugh always told me: "If we are ever robbed, don't argue. Just do what you're told and give them whatever they want."

Lord only knew what they wanted. "Help you?" I managed to choke out.

They looked around and must have figured I was alone. They surrounded me. One of them blocked the door. The biggest thug flashed a cruel grin. "Hey, mama," he sneered. "Got any specials?" The other two snorted.

"I'm sorry," I said. "We're closed. I was just cleaning up."

"Whadda ya mean, closed?" he snapped. He brought his face right up to mine. "It's Christmas," he said. "I need some flowers. Now!"

His breath reeked. I turned my head, nearly gagging. I saw Hugh coming from the back room. He stopped short, took in the situation, then quickly came to my side. "What do you need, fellas?" Hugh said. "Make it quick."

"Lookie here, another one," said the leader. "You're not closing yet. First I wanna see what you got." He looked around. "Let's see them shiny things up there." He pointed toward the vase-filled shelves high on the wall. "Come on, let's see 'em."

Hugh reached to get one down.

"Not that one. The one over there." He pointed to the far end of the shelf and cackled. Hugh walked over and had just started to take the vase down when the thug said, "Old man, can't you get anything right? I meant the red one, back there." This time he pointed to another shelf.

The other two stood close by me. No way they would let me make it to the phone, let alone the front door. The sun was down now. It was completely black. Please, God, show us a way out of this.

Hugh raced around the store, the three toying with him. They laughed harder and harder. Hugh got winded, disoriented. It seemed to go on forever. Suddenly Hugh stopped and shouted, "Enough! I've had enough!"

No, Hugh! Just do what they say.

"What do you mean 'enough,' old man?" the leader shouted. "We're just startin' to have fun, aren't we?" Suddenly all three converged on my husband. I ran to the phone.

At that moment the front door opened. A rush of cold winter air blew in. The thugs looked up. Two young men entered the shop. Both were neatly dressed in brown suits and hats. Each carried a briefcase. One of them walked over to the near-empty display case. The second walked up to the counter. Neither of them said a word.

In the silence, I felt a presence. My eardrums pounded from the overwhelming presence of strength and goodness. I glanced over at Hugh, untouched by the thugs. They seemed spellbound, frozen in mid-attack. They couldn't seem to take their eyes off the two mysterious young men.

Then I saw Hugh react, as if some power had struck him. He puffed up before my eyes. "You guys don't want anything," he yelled. "Quit jerking me around and get out of here!"

The thugs looked at Hugh, then at the two newcomers, who stared silently back. The tables had been turned. The menace in the hoodlums' eyes vanished and was replaced by fear. By sheer terror! They bolted for the door and disappeared back into the night.

I tried to collect myself, thanking our two saviors again and again. They didn't look identical, yet I could not help but think of them as twins.

"Do you have a white rose?" one asked. "Do you have a white rose?" repeated the other.

"I'm so sorry, no," I said. "Could I offer you a red one instead?"

They shook their heads no, said thank you and turned to leave.

Hugh followed them to the door, locked it behind them, then switched off the overhead lights. He reached out to me and I hugged him close, still trembling. It was a long time till I finally broke the silence. "Those young men . . ."

"Never saw them before in my life."

We knew everyone in town, all right, but it appeared that there were a few guardian angels we hadn't yet met.

A Simple Assignment

ZIBI DAVIDSON

This story isn't really about me, and it isn't really about Christmas. But it is about a little Christmas tree ornament I made. It began with an assignment I had given my seventh-grade English class, requiring them to explain a process. Doug, one of my students, took some joshing for his project—demonstrating how to make ribbon-and-lace angel ornaments—but they were exquisite. An avid angel collector myself, I made them for Christmas gifts that year.

Some time later, my friend Pat was asked to lead a retreat for our church. I couldn't attend the retreat, but I volunteered to make gifts for the closing party. With Doug's instructions by my side I fashioned sixty-five angels of satin ribbon, decorator pearls, and silk rosebuds to be given out as lapel pins.

I learned later that one of the participants, Kathleen Murphy, got home that evening to find her son was very sick. She rushed him to the hospital. The doctors said he would be fine. But in the next room there was a critically ill baby who was not expected to live through the night. The baby's mother, who had to go arrange for a babysitter for her other child, asked if Kathleen would keep an eye on her infant. And Kathleen, who had not even had time to change clothes, removed the angel ornament from her lapel and hung it on a mobile above the crib.

Later that night when the baby's mother saw the angel dangling over the crib, something awoke in her. Though she was not a religious woman, she was moved to pray for her child. In the morning she and the doctors were amazed. The baby had pulled through. And the young mother left the hospital with new faith in God's power and love.

So as I said, this story isn't really about me. It's about how a classroom assignment became part of a child's miraculous recovery, about the mysterious and wondrous link that connects us all in God's plan. This time, with the help of a tiny Christmas-tree angel, I saw my small part in that great plan.

The Blizzard of '82

ZARETTE BEARD

*I*t was Christmas Eve 1982. I was in high school and my only brother, Norm, was my best friend. He was quirky, funny, lovable, and loyal. He had graduated three years prior and was already out on his own. I missed having him around, especially during the holidays. I was still living at home in a suburb north of Denver. Norm was living in a suburb south of Denver. I begged, I mean really begged him to come home for Christmas. He promised he'd be there. I knew without a doubt, barring a natural disaster, he would be home. Did I say natural disaster?

As is typical in Colorado, it started to snow. And snow. And snow some more. The entire city shut down. No cars were allowed on the roads unless they were four-wheel drives on their way to provide emergency services. The snow was simply too deep.

I stared out the big picture window in the living room,

helplessly watching the snow pile up. The drifts were already up to the window, and it was truly a beautiful sight. I wish I could have enjoyed it, but my heart was as lonely and quiet as the empty streets. I sighed and went to my room to read. I was grateful that, at least in our end of town, the power was still on. I had just turned on another lamp to read when I heard a knock at the front door. I rolled my eyes, tossed my book onto the desk, and slowly headed for the front door, knowing full well it was yet another neighbor needing my energy and my shovel. I scolded myself for such a grinchy attitude at this time of year and decided to dig out whoever it was at my door.

I opened the door to the strangest thing I had ever seen. There stood a man, wearing snowboots with wadded-up newspapers sticking out of the tops and frozen jeans. Puffy sleeves peeked out from underneath a big trashbag disguised as a poncho. His hat had a thick layer of frost on it, but it was his face that was intriguing.

This man's face was red from the windburn with white patches from being so cold. His eyebrows and mustache had tiny icicles dangling from them. We regarded each other for just a moment when he broke the silence.

"Meh-he-ree Ca—rist-mas, Zarette!" the frozen man yelled.

Taken aback, I looked closer to see which one of my crazy

neighbors was at my door. And then I recognized something. Those eyes. Those soft, brown, caring eyes. I squealed in surprise and delight. "Norm! You're here!" I jumped into his arms and almost knocked him off the porch. He just laughed at me, the way he always did. He was so cold he could barely speak. I dragged him into the house and helped him remove layer after layer of frozen clothes. I made some hot chocolate, and we sat down. I asked him how he made it all the way to my home in this raging blizzard.

He explained that a promise is a promise and no blizzard was going to stand in his way. He simply bundled up and started walking. A sympathetic trucker and a kind man in a four-wheel drive gave him a lift. He simply got out and walked when they reached their destinations. It took him nine hours to reach me, but he did it and gave me one of the best Christmas memories I will ever have.

That was twenty-four years ago. My brother, Norm, spent this Christmas with me, and wouldn't you know, there was a blizzard. We looked at each other knowingly as we sipped hot chocolate together and watched the snow fall from the sky.

O Lord, Watch over These, Your Special Children

SYBIL ROBERTS CANON

A gray cheerless morning, two weeks before Christmas in 1981. There we were, thirty-two of us huddled against the chill, waiting for the fast-food restaurant to open. Washington, DC, had looked beautiful when we arrived the night before, with Christmas trees in every square and streetlights transformed into enchanted towers with twinkling lights and garlands. But now, looking at the cold, unlovely street dotted with X-rated movies and bars, I wished we had stopped for breakfast in a better section of town.

The group I was shepherding is called the Miracles, a traveling choir from the Baddour Center, in Senatobia, Mississippi. Baddour is a community for mildly retarded adults, and all twenty-five members of the choir were residents there. These special people all hold full-time paying jobs at the Center. Their tasks range from simple to quite complex, depending on their abilities, and their productivity is phenomenal. On weekends the Miracles travel to churches and halls all over Mississippi and neighboring states, giving concerts. In fact, they have sung in twenty-two states and Mexico. Invariably, audiences come away inspired and with new insights about the gifts and abilities of these "handicapped" adults.

This particular day, we were going to sing in the rotunda of the United States Senate Office Building. Then, after some sightseeing, we would be off to New York City to give a Christmas concert at Marble Collegiate Church on Fifth Avenue.

There were other people stomping in the cold with us, mostly street people, or so it seemed to me—men with unshaven chins who carried open bottles wrapped in brown bags, women with bulging shopping bags, and girls in miniskirts and too much make-up.

As the doors opened and we moved into the restaurant's welcome warmth, I noticed one particular girl for the first time. She was young, not more than eighteen or twenty, but she had a hard, frayed-around-the-edges look, as if she had already been used up by the city. She was wearing tight jeans and a short jacket of fake fur. Her arms, when she removed the jacket, were mottled with cold, because her skimpy blouse was for summer wear. Her shoes were backless clogs that clip-clopped when she walked. In a pathetic stab at glamour, she had pulled her not-too-clean hair to one side and fixed it with a large white artificial flower. It was obvious that she had been up all night. It seemed just as obvious, to me, why.

"Come on, Miracles," I called, motioning them to a group of tables along one wall. "Let's sit over there!"

Most people might think that traveling with and supervising a group of twenty-five retarded adults would be difficult. Not at all. The Miracles are a wonderful group who listen to instructions, cooperate beautifully, and maintain a happy, positive attitude. But ordering breakfast for the Miracles is not quite so easy. At last, however, I got the list straight—I think: 22 orange juices, 16 milks, 14 orders of pancakes, 14 coffees, seven Egg McMuffins and five scrambled eggs with sausage. And after one or two spilled coffees and juices, we settled down to eat.

As usual, we got our share of stares from other people, and I knew it wasn't because we were all dressed alike in our spiffy new red blazers with the Baddour insignia on the breast pockets. No, people always stare, because they see the Miracles are different.

I was heading back for the last of our coffees when the girl with the fake fur reached out and touched my arm. "Hey . . . who are you all?"

I looked into her tired eyes, red-rimmed and caked with too much mascara. "We're called the Miracles," I replied, and I explained that we were on tour and were headed for New York City. The girl, meanwhile, was twisting a cigarette in her fingers. "That's real nice," she replied, looking at the Miracles with unabashed curiosity.

I came back with the coffee and sat down with Ruth, our bus driver's wife.

"What was that all about?" Ruth asked, looking at the girl with as much curiosity as the girl had looked at our group.

"She just wanted to know who we are," I replied, buttering my pancakes. I was just in the act of raising my fork to my mouth when I looked again at the girl sitting at an empty table. Not even a coffee cup . . . and she looked hungry.

I put my fork down. On impulse I went to the counter and asked for another order of pancakes, sausages, and coffee. "How about having breakfast with the Miracles?" I said to the girl as casually as I could, putting the tray in front of her. She was flustered, unsure of how to react, and then, even without my saying anything to them, the Miracles began drifting over toward her.

Richard and Thornton, Nancy and Audrey, Jeanna and David—they all brought their trays and sat down near her. Soon all of them were talking animatedly, forks waving, the girl laughing. "Can you believe that?" I said to Ruth.

Nancy, who is the receptionist at Baddour, was giving the girl a Baddour Center Who's Who: "Richard Hollie here doesn't read a note of music," Nancy was saying with pride, "but he's a concert pianist. And this is Thornton Chisom, our lead singer. He's got the greatest voice!"

"You sing?" the girl asked Thornton, puffing on her cigarette. "I always wanted to be a singer." Then she looked off into space and said, "I'm from Texas."

"Are you? So am I!" Thornton exclaimed, beaming.

When we had finished eating, we collected ourselves and started to leave. We were all feeling good, Thornton especially, for as he got to the door, he turned and began singing. "Come On, Ring Those Bells," he sang in his rich baritone. Then the rest of us joined in. The people in the restaurant, at tables, and behind counters, gaped, first in astonishment, then in pleasure. There we were, in our trim red blazers, singing happily away. And, to my great surprise, I saw that the girl had joined the group. There she was, right in the middle of us, this gawky girl in her tight jeans and sloppy clogs, trying to sing along and grin at the same time.

We finished our song, and the restaurant burst into applause and cheers. A grizzled old man croaked, "Merry Christmas to all!" waving his brown paper bag.

Jeanna, who has Down's syndrome, turned to the girl and said, "You come and see us at Baddour. Okay?"

"I will! I will!" the girl said happily.

"Merry Christmas!" the Miracles called out, pushing through the door into the December air.

On the bus I made the head count. Something was wrong; I checked again. Then I discovered why there was one too many. The girl had boarded the bus too.

"Hey, Miracles!" she called out. "Do you know 'Silent Night'?"

"Sure we know that!" I said. But glancing out of the bus windows, I saw that the morning rush-hour traffic was already clogging the street. We would have to move the bus. *Well, the cars can just wait a minute!* I told myself as I raised my hands.

"Si-a-lent night, h-o-o-ly night . . ." the sweet voices sang in unison. The last notes of the beloved old carol died away, amid the sounds of honking horns and motors.

"Thank you, Miracles . . . thank you!" the girl said almost in a whisper as she got off the bus. She ran quickly to the center island of the busy street, then turned and waved. We all crowded to the windows, waving back until the bus turned the corner.

As we drove to the Senate Office Building for our concert, I looked around. The Miracles—Jeanna, Audrey, Richard, Thornton, Douglas, Nancy, and the others—were chattering away, looking at the store windows and the streets beginning to crowd with holiday shoppers. By now the Miracles had forgotten the girl, but I couldn't get the picture of her out of my mind—standing there on that traffic island, smiling and waving.

The Miracles had touched her, I knew that, touched her with their friendliness, their innocence, touched her because they, too, were different. And for just a moment my mind's eye saw this girl who wanted to be a singer going home again, home for Christmas to some little town in Texas where she could begin to live and dream again.

Lord, I prayed in my heart, as the bus crawled through traffic, *please watch over this Your child, whoever she is, wherever she goes. Watch over her as You've watched over these Your special children who have their own special gifts to give.*

The bus lurched to a stop. Looking through the window I saw the letters carved on the building: Offices of the Senate of the United States.

"Okay, Miracles!" I called. "We're here. Everybody out!"

All My Heart, This Night Rejoices

JUDY STANFIELD CORLEY

I parked in the nearly deserted lot and started toward the hospital entrance, my open coat flapping in the freezing wind. I wanted to feel the cold air on my neck, wanted the snow promised by the imposing mass of gray clouds overhead to pour down on me—anything to break through the numbing grief I'd felt for the last two years.

That Christmas Eve I was on my way to comfort my friend Naomi. Her only child, twelve-year-old Jimmy, had slipped into a coma despite a brave fight with cancer. Naomi had been my first friend in Nashville. My husband, Bob, and I had moved there eight months earlier. Living in Naomi's apartment building, we saw a lot of her. When I listened to her play her guitar and sing, I felt an inkling of peace.

I walked up the hospital steps, slipping on the icy slush, and took the elevator to the children's floor. A large tree with blinking lights and shiny ornaments stood in the lobby. The nurse's station was lined with food baskets from grateful families. A radio softly played Christmas music. *Why even bother?* I thought to myself. The display seemed pointless in the face of the sadness and suffering all around.

I walked into Jimmy's darkened room. Tubes protruded from all over his body, and his breathing was labored. A heart monitor beeped. Christmas cards decorated the wall opposite his bed. Naomi stood at the window, her guitar resting on the chair behind her. I went over and hugged her.

"Where is everybody?" I asked. Naomi's relatives had been taking turns sitting with Jimmy.

"They're taking a break. Weren't you and Bob going to a Christmas party?"

"I didn't feel like celebrating. And I thought you could use some company."

She smiled at me in the dimness, then closed her eyes. I looked out at the clouds hanging low in the sky, so thick they made the heavens seem impenetrable, even to prayer. I doubted God was listening anyway. Hadn't my pleas for a child of my own gone unanswered?

I thought of the crib Bob and I had so carefully picked out, the toys tucked away on the top shelf in our closet, the baby names I had whispered to myself, longing to call them out loud. Two years earlier when I became pregnant, I was thrilled. But then came the spring day when my doctor sadly told me the baby I had carried for eight months was dead. Later, he told me a second pregnancy was unlikely. I didn't think anyone could ease the loneliness I felt every time I looked at that empty crib, waiting for something that would never be. It seemed a cruel irony that, on this night celebrating the birth of a child, I was still mourning my son and Naomi was losing hers. So much for Christmas miracles.

Naomi picked up her guitar from the chair. She held it, strumming thoughtfully. Then she began to sing "What Child Is This?" her clear, sweet voice filling the room. I sat beside the bed and held Jimmy's hand in mine. *I wish we could get through to you, Jimmy,* I thought. *Come back to us.*

Looking over at Naomi, I saw the doorway was crowded with people listening to her song. A woman stood behind a little boy in a wheelchair, stroking his hair. A man carried a baby girl with IVs attached to her arms and feet. Other children peeked around the edges of the doorway. Naomi got up and walked into the hallway, still singing. I heard her going up and down the corridor, her voice ringing out with warmth and joy even in the midst of her own sorrow. I kept holding tight to Jimmy's hand, wishing I could give so much of myself to others. But I felt hollow, spent. I had nothing to give.

Jimmy stirred a bit, moaning softly. Outside, the night looked dark and brooding. If only something would happen. I was so tired of waiting for things. For a child of my own, for Jimmy to wake up, for the snow to fall . . .

Naomi came back with a nurse, who checked the machines connected to Jimmy. "His vital signs are steady but weak," she said to Naomi. "If he doesn't wake up soon . . ." Her voice trailed off.

The nurse left, closing the door behind her. Naomi buried her head in the sheets beside Jimmy. I felt her sorrow so deeply it pushed aside my own for a moment. "God," I whispered, "please help."

The door opened and I looked up, expecting to see the nurse again. Instead, Naomi's family filed into the room. I stepped back toward the window as they circled the bed and reached out to touch Jimmy's frail body. A blanket of hands, young and old, smooth and gnarled, moved over him. His grandmother lay down beside him and whispered into his ear. Naomi began to play her guitar again.

"All my heart this night rejoices," she and her family sang. "As I hear, far and near, sweetest angel voices."

I'd never heard the song before. It was beautiful. Naomi's brother turned to me, stretching out his hand. I hesitated, but he nodded and smiled. I grasped his hand and stepped into their circle. When I reached out for their hands, I felt God reaching out to me through my shell of numbness and filling the emptiness inside me with hope. There was no blinding light, no thunder, no shaking of the earth. But in that moment I felt my wintertime ending. When I glanced out into the night, snow was falling at last.

Everyone except Naomi stopped singing. Blinking back tears, I looked down at Jimmy. All at once, he opened his eyes. "Sing 'O Holy Night,' Mama," he said hoarsely. Without a pause, as if she had been expecting it all along, Naomi started singing the song. The rest of her family embraced one another and me. Wrapped in their arms, I listened to the peal of distant church bells. They seemed to be singing in celebration of Jimmy's awakening. And my own.

I went home to celebrate Christmas with my husband,

knowing I had already received the gift I really needed. For the first time in two years, I felt part of the world again. God had been waiting for me to come back to Him as we had waited for Jimmy to come back to us. I saw then that whatever the future held, He would be there beside me.

Today, twenty-two years later, I'm reminded of that every time I reach out for the hands of my three sons. Through them, God embraces me with His love—as He did that snowy Christmas Eve when my heart learned to rejoice again.

And by the way, Jimmy eventually returned home and his cancer went into remission.

Christmas Miracles

CONNIE WILCOX

All month long I have been saying, "It is time for miracles." The holiday season always brings surprises, joy, and generosity.

Working at Longmont's transitional housing facility called the Inn Between, I have witnessed these miracles for years. Anonymous donors and community support miraculously appear to help the Inn's many residents. I have the honor of watching people's tears of joy and relief when something they are in need of appears. I see their gratefulness for the help, and the instant renewal to their spirit. Donna Lovato, the Inn's executive director, attributes it to the Inn's angels. When a tenant needs something, Donna just asks the angels to bring it to the Inn. Within a few days, sometimes sooner, it appears. I am fortunate to work in a place where I get to see miracles happen every day!

Last week, one of the largest miracles I have seen

occurred at the Inn. One of the residents was in desperate need of a thousand dollars to get her car fixed. She was very distraught over the high repair quote. An anonymous donor appeared at our door wanting to donate money for this specific tenant. We graciously accepted the donation and worked quickly to pass it on to the tenant. The tenant was called to the office where we presented her with a check for the thousand dollars. She was shocked, amazed, grateful, shaking, and full of tears. By the time she left, the entire staff was in tears as well.

This year, I not only witnessed a grand miracle, I experienced one firsthand. My family has been struggling financially. For the past several months, the bills have exceeded our income to the point where buying groceries was a luxury. My husband and I both work, and run a retail Internet business on evenings and weekends. We both have been putting in long days trying to keep up with the increasing costs of survival. I am stubborn, proud, and self-sufficient. I have always worked and done whatever it took to keep my family going. We don't live extravagantly, but we are happy with what we have. Our house is a thousand square feet, our newest car is twelve years old, and our cell phones don't take pictures. I thought I felt gratitude for the things I do have, but I realized that I had no idea what being grateful really felt like.

When my neighbor Judy asked the innocent question, "Do you have all of your holiday shopping done?" I laughed and said, "Well, maybe I can buy groceries out of my next check, then Christmas presents with the one after that.

We continued our conversation about our health, stress, and kids, and I didn't give it another thought, until today. Her son came by our house to drop off a Christmas card. I opened the card and two grocery store gift cards tumbled onto the floor! I picked them up thinking, *Oh, how sweet.* Then I saw that they were in the amount of five hundred dollars each. I started crying and shaking and saying, "Oh, thank God!" over and over. I didn't know what to do. I think I had a mini panic attack after that.

I tried calling her immediately to tell her that I couldn't possibly accept such a large gift. She wasn't home. I tried to think of what to say to her. While my thoughts were reeling, it occurred to me that my own miracle had just occurred. Last week, while I was working at the Inn, I had asked the angels for a Christmas miracle. I knew that I would need one to make it through the holidays.

I did get to talk with Judy a little later. She explained that she had experienced a similar situation and that someone had helped her out. Her family had a really prosperous year, and they wanted to share it with others. Still overwhelmed, I am feeling better about accepting the gift. I have been crying all afternoon, feeling humble, relieved, and grateful. This experience has shown me that the pay-it-forward idea really can work!

I never thought I would be in a position where I would have to rely on someone else to make it. It is a new and eye-opening experience to be on the same side as those I work to help every day. I thought I understood what they were going through, when I really had no idea. What an enlightening experience. It made me realize that if it happened to me, it could happen to any one of us. During the five years I have worked at the Inn, I have always said that most people are just one paycheck away from needing to live there. Today, I realized just how truthful that statement is.

I will never forget the feeling I have today. This experience has made a deep imprint on my soul that will not be forgotten. I will remember to share when I can, and to think of how much impact you can have by helping others. I thank Judy and Terry for their generous spirit and hope that they realize how thankful I am. Their generosity not only makes an enormous difference in my life today but for many years to come. I give thanks to the Inn's angels for bringing me a Christmas miracle.

CHAPTER 2

Yuletide Mysteries

The virgin will be pregnant. She will have a son, and they will name him Immanuel, which means "God is with us" (Matthew 1:23).

The mysteries of Christmas are many. How did the infinite Son of God stuff Himself into the tiny, finite body of a human baby? How did the perfect, sinless Savior live in this imperfect, sin-filled world? How did the star in the East just suddenly appear in the sky? How did the wise men in the East manage to follow that star to the very house where the Christ Child lived? And how can we—impure, unholy, unclean—be so blessed as to be saved from ourselves by a holy God and His majestic Son? What mysteries! What blessings!

Act of Faith

RICHARD H. SCHNEIDER

As the cab threaded its way through Manhattan's East Side, I wondered about the man I was about to meet. Gian Carlo, the well-known composer, was a stranger to me, though I knew his works well, especially his opera *Amahl and the Night Visitors.*

Along with millions of others around the world, I had been captivated by its beautiful story in which a crippled little boy and his careworn mother are among the first to experience the love and healing power of the newborn Christ. Seen on television annually, it is reported to be the most popular Christmas music offering, next to Handel's *Messiah.*

But of its composer I knew little. Bits and pieces of his life gleaned from news clips and articles intrigued me. I was especially struck by one reference to something unusual, even mystical, behind the inspiration of this opera.

Fascinated, I wrote him regarding a visit. It took fifteen months to come about. When he isn't composing, which is almost always, the maestro is traveling the world overseeing musical events, such as the Spoleto Festivals in Italy and Charleston, South Carolina.

But now my cab drew up in front of the apartment building where he lives when in New York. A small elevator creaked to his floor, and I stepped out into the hall to be welcomed by the composer.

A lean man with penetrating eyes, he ushered me into his living room, where eighteenth-century prints and marble statuary evoked a gracious Italian atmosphere. Now in his seventieth year, he spoke enthusiastically of his love of composing: "It is my life." When our talk turned to *Amahl,* his eyes twinkled, he leaned back, and in his soft Italian accent told me the story behind the opera.

It all began, he said, in the New York Metropolitan Museum of Art. It was the fall of 1951 and Gian Carlo Menotti wandered gloomily through the museum, trying to take his troubled mind off the responsibility that was tormenting him.

Why did I ever sign that contract? he wondered. A few years earlier, the National Broadcasting Company had asked him to compose a one-act opera for television. Since he had already written several well-received productions and had fulfilled commissions for everything from ballets to operas, the assignment seemed perfectly feasible. He accepted a one-thousand-dollar advance payment and agreed to submit the opera in time for a Christmas production in 1951.

But for some reason, he could not come up with a story. He tried and tried, discarding theme after theme. Finally, giving up, he wrote to Samuel Chotzinoff, head of the NBC opera company, and asked if he could return the advance money and withdraw from the assignment.

The NBC people called him in, concerned. "We don't want the money," they pleaded. "We want your opera." They persuaded Gian Carlo to try once more.

He did, again and again, but still could not come up with an idea that inspired him. Not only did he feel he was disappointing other people, but he wondered if his creative powers might be waning.

Now it was late fall and, seeking respite from his misery, he had entered the Metropolitan Museum. Wearily he climbed the stairs to its second floor and walked into a gallery with a collection of European masterpieces from the fourteenth to the eighteenth centuries. Then something about one of them caught his eye, and he paused.

The work was *The Adoration of the Three Kings* by Hieronymus Bosch, a fifteenth-century Dutch painter. Highlighted in the center of walled ruins was the Virgin Mary with the Baby Jesus in her lap. A shepherd knelt nearby. Three kings, robed in regal glory, offered the Child sumptuous gifts.

It was the kings that had caught Gian Carlo Menotti's eye. They reminded him of Christmas celebrations in his childhood home in Cadegliano, Italy. Italian children at that time did not receive their holiday gifts from Santa Claus. Instead, the gifts were left by the Wise Men as they traveled toward Bethlehem on the eve of Epiphany, January 6.

Gian Carlo smiled, recalling how he and his little brother Tullio looked forward to that night. They had tried so hard to stay awake to see the royal visitors. And though they never succeeded, it always seemed to Gian Carlo that just before he fell asleep he could hear them coming—the eerie cadence of their song in the distant blue hills, the camels' hooves crunching the snow of northern Italy, the jingling of the silver bridles.

In that quiet museum gallery, he again heard coming from the distant hills of his childhood the haunting music of the Three Kings. With the flame of an idea kindled, he went home to work. Composing to the maestro is an essential part of his daily life. He composes while shaving, eating, taking a walk . . .

Undoubtedly, he mused as he worked, the Three Kings had stopped at many houses during their long journey. Those ruins he had seen in the Bosch painting—perhaps someone was living there? Perhaps a poor widow and her child . . . a little boy? The composer decided to call him Amahl after a name he dimly remembered from a childhood book.

He began to jot down ideas for the words, and the words immediately suggested some music, the sound of distant singing as the kings wound their way down from the hills. What were they like, these royal personages?

Again his mind ranged back to childhood; his favorite then had been Melchior, because he was the oldest and had a long, white beard. His brother's favorite was Kaspar. Tullio insisted that this king was a little crazy and quite deaf—possibly because Kaspar never brought Tullio all the gifts he asked for!

As the characters took form, Gian Carlo let NBC know that he was on to something. Immediately he was sorry. Though he had no idea how the opera would take shape, the television network confidently made plans to present it live on Christmas Eve.

That was only a month away!

There was so much to do in developing the story.

Who was the little boy Amahl? he wondered. *What was he like?* He gazed out his studio window and thought about himself. Here he was, a forty-year-old man whose childhood dreams, as the poet Wordsworth put it, had "faded into the light of common day." Lost with his dreams was a belief in such wonders as three kings who brought children gifts on Epiphany. *What had happened,* he wondered, *to the faith of little Gian Carlo who had believed so completely?*

And then he remembered something special about his young beliefs. It had been so long ago he had almost forgotten . . . At age four, he was lame. The doctors could not cure what they called a "white tumor" in his leg, and it was difficult for him to walk.

In his household there in Cadegliano was a person of great faith, his governess called Maria. She came from peasant stock and was adored by all the children in the family because of her incredible patience and sweetness. She was also blessed with great faith in God, which gave her surprising strength and understanding. Maria knew of a church high in the nearby Lugano mountains, the Madonna del Monte, where it was said God worked miracles. She asked him, "Gian Carlo, do you believe God can heal you?"

He nodded in earnest conviction.

And so his dear Maria took him into the mountains to the place of God. And he was healed.

The doctors had no explanation why Gian Carlo was able to walk again. But Maria believed, and he believed. And the healing came.

Now, as the maestro gazed out his studio window, a picture began forming in his mind. It was the boy Amahl leaning on a crude wooden crutch. Of course! He was lame, as Gian Carlo had been. He needed a healing. And the story would be the miracle of the healing that comes when Amahl offers his crutch as a gift to the Christ Child.

Days and nights blurred into an endless penciling of notes and orchestration, of crumpling music sheets and starting over again.

Rehearsals in New York City were already underway and, feverishly writing a few pages at a time, Menotti gave them to his cook to rush to the railroad station where NBC couriers picked them up.

The excitement. The frustration. The exhaustion. Until finally one morning, with the green-shaded desk lamp still burning as his frosted studio windows glowed pink with the rising sun, Gian Carlo Menotti leaned back in his chair, totally spent. *Amahl and the Night Visitors* was a reality. The opera was finished.

"Inspiration," says Menotti reflectively, "how can one define it?"

I am still in the maestro's Manhattan living room. Menotti continues speaking: "It is as if God would send you a momentary flash of total recall—but a recall of what?" His eyes search beyond me.

"Both St. Augustine and Plato have spoken of beauty as 'divine perfection,'" he resumes. "Only a few lucky artists can achieve that state of grace that allows them to have a fleeting glimpse of this beauty." He is silent for a moment, then adds, "Was I one of the lucky ones? Perhaps I was."

The Gift of the Hummingbird

MARILYN A. KINSELLA

*H*ummingbirds are fascinating little creatures. They whirl around with flashes of iridescent colors. Their elongated beaks swish the air like miniature swords. They maneuver the skies with the ease of stealth bombers. Sometimes they appear out of the corner of your eye and then disappear in a radiant arc.

My mother believed in pixies and fairy dust. She had an imagination that made shadows dance on the wall at night. During the day she could make petunias twirl around in their ball gowns. Her mother had beautiful gardens around the house and, while not helping with the chores, Mom spent many an hour playing in the gardens. It was her magical place.

Her favorite spot was right underneath the front porch. That's where she and her brother, Les, used to hide and wait for the hummingbirds. The tiny birds were attracted by the big, bright red flowers her mother planted along the side of the house. She and Les positioned themselves under the porch for a perfect hideaway. They could see out, but the hummingbirds couldn't see in. A lattice border was all that separated them from the little hummers. Their chubby faces shone like a checkerboard of diamonds. They looked out anxiously. She and Les became very quiet. About four o'clock, they could hear a faint, distant hum. Then they came—a squadron of green, winged leprechauns dive-bombing out of the sky and into the hearts of the red flowers. Invariably, they felt a giggle bubbling up, so they put their hands over their mouths. Now the giggles came out in a series of chortles and chuffs. Curious, one of the hummers might peer inside with its black, beady eyes. Then, in a wink . . . it was gone.

Looking back I guess that's why my mom always had a fascination with hummingbirds. When they became fashionable as gifts in the early eighties, Mom and I gave each other hummingbirds. It might be something rather silly like thermometers and potholders or something sublime like sun catchers and delicate crystalline hummingbirds. Candleholders, plates, music boxes, scarves, paintings—if it had a hummingbird, we bought it for each other.

Our birthdays were only four hours apart. So, we

often shared our birthday celebrations on the same day. We laughed hysterically when one year we gave each other the very same gold, hummingbird pin. Mom especially liked the "anything" cards with our favorite bird on it. Inside I'd write some trite poetry that made her laugh.

That's why I asked her to send me a hummingbird after she died. Mom died in October of 1997. I carried a guilty feeling for having to place her in a nursing home. Looking back I still think it was the best solution to a very difficult situation, but that didn't make my decision any easier, especially when she didn't want to be there.

So, that November, when I was crying alone in my bedroom, I said out loud, "Mom, I want you to send me a hummingbird. It will be a sign of forgiveness and that you are in a much happier place. And, by the way, hummingbirds are hard to find this time of year, so I'll know if I get one, it will be from you."

Well, days, and weeks went by and no hummingbird. Even on Christmas Eve I remember thinking, *I guess she's still mad.*

Then on Christmas morning, I must have had twenty gifts at my feet. As per our family tradition, I selected one to open first as did the rest of my family. At the appointed moment we all opened the first gift of Christmas, and there it was . . . a beautiful crystal hummingbird that sat on a flowered stem. At first I was speechless, then I started to cry. My family was a bit puzzled. Why was I getting so emotional over a hummingbird?

Finally I blubbered out, "You don't understand. It's from my mom. I asked her to send me a hummingbird."

My husband, Larry, actually purchased the gift. He believes that a coincidence is a coincidence is a coincidence. That's why they coined the word *coincidence.*

But he said, "I don't mean to lend credence to what you're thinking, but it was a bit odd. I had already bought your toaster and showerhead and thought I should buy you something pretty. Suddenly, I thought of a hummingbird."

"See," I said, "you were listening!"

"No, I was desperate."

"Well," I countered, "you may have been desperate, but you were also listening."

Then he added, "But the really odd thing was, I had a hard time finding a hummingbird. I went to four or five stores before I found one on a kiosk."

"I know, because hummingbirds are hard to find this time of year." If I needed another sign that the hummingbird was from Mom, that was it.

Christmas Tag Miracle

MARY HOLLINGSWORTH

$\mathcal{M}$y dad was a minister. That meant I was a preacher's kid (PK). And while some PKs did not like living in glass houses, it never bothered me. The flip side of that coin is that we never had much money, because Dad primarily ministered to smaller churches in East and Central Texas. So I learned to work for additional spending money early in life. In fact, it all started one Christmas when I was in the third grade.

As a third-grader, Christmas was an exciting time of anticipation and planning. Because we were not abundantly blessed financially, we had to be inventive about the presents we gave. So I began pestering Mom in September about how I could earn some money to buy Christmas presents. Being an extremely creative lady, Mom came up with an interesting idea.

Mom invented a way to use old Christmas cards to

make unique Christmas tags to avoid paying for tags at the store. She would cut out one or two Christmas icons from the face of a card—a bell, a star, a pretty package, or an ornament—moving the scissors back and forth to create a scalloped edge around them. Then she would punch a hole in one corner of the cut-out tag. Next, she tied green or red yarn through the hole so the tag could be attached to a package. And *voilà!* She had a beautiful, original tag for her gift.

This particular year, Mom suggested we start making tags early and perhaps I could sell a few of them to neighbors or friends. So we asked our friends and family if they had old Christmas cards we could have, and they happily gave them to us. Then night after night Mom and I worked. By November we had hundreds of delightful, colorful Christmas tags ready to tempt Christmas shoppers.

Mom found a beautiful old wooden cigar box that was long, narrow, and thin, covered in pink satin fabric, with a hinged lid and an attached ribbon that kept the lid from falling back too far. I put as many tags as would fit into the box, and out the door I went to sell my wares. A half-dozen tags cost thirty cents; a full dozen was sixty cents.

Surprisingly, our neighbors and friends were delighted with the handmade tags. So little by little my Christmas money built up until the third week of December when I had about twenty dollars—a veritable fortune for a third-grader in 1954.

The last day I planned to sell tags, I was walking down the street to an area of our neighborhood I had not yet visited when I met a pretty lady I'd never seen before on our street. She smiled at me, and I said, "Hello."

Then she paused and said, "Mary, don't forget to stop at Mrs. Walker's house with your Christmas tags today."

Since I didn't know the lady, I was surprised that she knew my name, knew about my tags, and knew Mrs. Walker. So I just mumbled, "Okay, I won't." And I walked on slowly, looking back over my shoulder to try and remember who she was. She smiled at me again and waved good-bye as she went on her way.

Mrs. Walker was well known by the kids in our neighborhood, because she had a funny parrot named Clipper that stayed in a cage in her garage. Mrs. Walker left the garage door open most of the time, and Clipper jabbered and talked to anyone who came near.

Before I met the lady on the street, I had decided not to ask Mrs. Walker to buy my Christmas tags. Her husband had died in early November, and I didn't want to bother her. However, after the woman told me not to forget her, I somehow felt compelled to call on Mrs. Walker.

Walking into the familiar garage, I said, "Hello, Clipper."

"Hello! Hello!" he squawked.

I knocked on the door as softly as I could. Then I heard Mrs. Walker coming to the door.

"Well, Mary, I'm so glad to see you. Please come in."

"Thank you, Mrs. Walker. How are you doing?"

"Well, darlin', I'm doing all right. But you look as if you've got something to show me. What's in your box?"

"They're Christmas tags. I thought you might like to buy a few to put on your Christmas gifts, especially since some of them were made from the cards you gave us."

"Well, let's just take a look here," she smiled, sitting down in her favorite rocking chair in the den. And she began looking through the tags, one by one, as if she were searching for something in particular.

As she got toward the bottom of the stack of tags, suddenly her breath caught in her throat. And as she pulled out one of the larger, more oranate tags, a tear trickled down her cheek.

"Mrs. Walker, are you okay? Did I do something to make you sad?" I asked.

"No, sweetheart. In fact, you've just done something to make me very happy. You see, when I gave you my old

Christmas cards for your business, I didn't realize I had given you the card my husband gave to me last Christmas—the last Christmas card I'll ever get from him. When I discovered what I'd done, I didn't want to ask for it back; so I just thought I'd never see it again. But this tag was made from that very special card—I'd know it anywhere."

"Oh! I'm so sorry we cut up your card. We had no idea . . ."

"Now, don't you worry," she said with a smile. "You did exactly the right thing. You see, my husband had already bought my Christmas present for this year, but he hadn't put a name tag on it yet. So I will just use this tag on his gift to me and open it on Christmas morning, just as we always did. Nothing could be more perfect."

After picking out several more tags, Mrs. Walker paid me sixty cents, but I would not let her pay me for that one very special tag. Then I gave her a hug, wished her merry Christmas, and left through the garage door.

"Good-bye, Clipper!" I said.

"See you later! See you later!" he quipped.

My Christmas tag business continued along quite well over the next few years. Our neighbors, friends, and family began calling us in October each year wanting to be sure I would be selling the tags again, because they liked the unique, homemade ones so much better than the cookie-cutter, store-bought ones. Now, each year I still send my mom my old Christmas cards, because she still makes her own Christmas tags to this day.

I've often wondered who that lady on the street was—a stranger, a neighbor, a friend of Mrs. Walker's, an angel? I'll never really know, but I do know what I prefer to believe. And I know a miracle when I see one, even one as small as a Christmas tag.

Learning Christmas Love

PAT J. SIKORA

Of all the Christmas gifts I've ever received, a simple doll from more than fifty years ago remains most treasured in my mind. It taught me a lesson I've never forgotten.

My parents, who owned a small, rundown motel in rural Wyoming, counted on the summer tourist season to carry us through the long, isolated winters. But few tourists had visited our area that summer, meaning that even covering the necessities was next to impossible. As the eldest of four children, I was old enough to understand my parents' dilemma, but young enough to grieve at the thought of a Christmas even more sparse than usual. While my friends were anticipating sleek bicycles, walking dolls, and stylish new clothes, I knew that my gifts would be far simpler. Meanwhile, the younger children continued to expect Santa to fill the gap they knew Mom and Dad couldn't.

Across the street from us was a dilapidated two-room shack. The peeling once-white paint barely covered a dwelling so small and inadequate that it was usually vacant. But that winter it housed the Miller family. We were delighted since the four Miller children were each slightly younger than each of us, making for great play-mates. However, we'd quickly learned that their life was much different than ours. Their father was long gone—where, they didn't know—and their mother worked long hours at the local café. I don't remember ever seeing her. The children were usually alone.

As the days of early December passed, my brother and sisters whispered of what Santa would bring us. Soon even I was excited enough to join in. Our faith in him was firm, even though Mom and Dad kept insisting that Santa had had a rough year too. I think we somehow felt that if we believed hard enough, he would come through.

And in fact, "he" always did. Despite many lean years, our parents had always managed to make Christmas special, filling the holiday with excitement and inexpensive but meaningful gifts to delight our hearts. Perhaps most important, in the midst of our poverty, we had one precious commodity that money couldn't buy—hope.

Not so with the Miller children. When they spoke of

Christmas, there was no excitement, no mystery, no expectation. Flatly, without anticipation, they insisted, "Santa isn't coming to our house this year."

At first we didn't believe them. Who ever heard of Santa totally skipping a family? But when we realized they were serious, our skepticism turned to distress. They weren't even sure they would be able to stay in their little home through the winter.

"How can they have no Christmas?" we quizzed our mother at lunch one day. All she could do was shrug sadly in reply. Dad had no answers either.

We fretted over their dilemma. We wished we could be Santa to the Millers. But of course that was out of the question. We had no money and our parents certainly didn't need another worry. We pondered for days trying to figure out what to do.

Then one night just days before Christmas, Dad came up with the most absurd idea we had ever heard of. Since Santa wouldn't be visiting the Millers, he proposed that maybe we children should.

"If you really care about your friends," he explained quietly, "your giving needs to be a sacrifice rather than something that doesn't cost you anything. Even if Mom and I could afford to help you, it wouldn't mean anything to you. You'll be getting a few gifts from relatives this year. So why not give one to each of your friends?"

He couldn't be serious! But he was. We didn't know what to say. We considered his idea for a long time—several days as I recall. We'd be receiving so little ourselves that the thought of giving even one precious gift away was heart-wrenching. But we knew that the Millers expected nothing at all.

Once we had made our decision, we could barely keep our secret as we anticipated the joy our gifts would bring. But at the same time, we had second—and third—thoughts. The suspense was unbearable. What precious gift would we lose? What if we regretted the decision? What if the cost was too high? Maybe Santa would come to the Millers after all, so we didn't really need to do this. Maybe it wasn't too late to change our minds.

But we had committed ourselves to the plan, and our dad saw to it that we carried through. As we opened our gifts that Christmas Eve, a little doll dressed in a bright blue dress and hat was among my small stack of presents—a gift from my favorite uncle. I held it close for a long minute, gave its hair a lingering stroke . . . and then carefully wrapped it in bright paper.

The cold wind whipped our thin coats and bit at our

cheeks and noses as we stepped out into the freshly fallen snow that night. Stars twinkled in the clear sky, and the streetlights turned the icy crystals into a carpet of diamonds. Across the street, the Miller house stood in darkness, a forlorn contrast to our mood.

Excitedly we crept across to the Miller's, new snow crunching under each step. At their doorstep we silently deposited a big bag tied with a red bow right in front of the door. Inside were that doll, a fighter plane from my brother, and stuffed animals from my sisters. The tag on the ribbon read simply, "Merry Christmas, Love Santa." Then we walked the short block to church to celebrate the Nativity, which became real to us for perhaps the first time.

As we ushered in Christmas moments later in our simple country church, I couldn't help thinking how surprised and delighted the Miller children would be when they discovered their presents. They would know that someone loved them, someone remembered them.

I don't remember any of the other presents I received that year, but I'll always remember the lessons I learned about giving. Not just giving useless gifts to people who don't need them, but really giving. I learned that true giving is motivated by love and often by sacrifice, just as two thousand yeas ago love motivated the Father to give His only Son to a needy world. And Christmas giving is as fresh today as it was that star-filled night in Bethlehem.

When I Opened My Eyes

PAT CIDDIO

*C*hristmas is the season of surprises. I mean surprise in the deepest sense of the word—the miracle of the unexpected. The kind of miracle that happened to me one Christmas. Not once, but twice.

Christmas Eve 2001, I was working at my daughter Susanne's jewelry stand at a Denver-area mall. The holidays were her busiest time, so I gave her a hand. It did me good too. With the carols playing over the public address system, the decorations in the store windows and the festive crowds, it was hard to feel lonely at the mall.

Not like at home. The house seemed a rather lonesome little corner of the world this time of year without my husband, John. He'd passed away thirteen years earlier, yet there wasn't a day that I didn't think about him. Miss him. I yearned for a connection to him, to his side of the family, even though I knew any hope of that was long gone. John's siblings had died well before him, as had his cousin Ralph from Italy, and we'd completely lost track of their children.

Susanne glanced up from the other side of the stand, where she was rearranging the bracelets, and smiled at me. I felt my longing give way to gratitude. For the wonderful life John and I had built together, for our children and grandchildren. A person couldn't really expect more blessings than that, could she?

Suddenly a wave of dizziness swept over me. I sat down heavily on the stool by the register. Susanne, still fiddling with the bracelet display, hadn't seen me falter. Good, since she'd only worry. My head cleared, and I got to work on polishing some silver charms in a display.

Another wave of dizziness. Worse this time. I gripped the edge of the stand.

Susanne dashed to my side. "Mom, are you okay?"

"I'm fine," I said, brushing her off.

She frowned. "I don't know, Mom," she said. "I'd rather close up early and take you home."

Two women came up, admiring the gold necklaces. "Why don't you take care of those customers?" I said to Susanne. "I'll be all right. This will pass."

I felt better by the time the mall closed. Still, Susanne wasn't taking any chances. She had to go home to her daughter, so she asked her brother, Tom, to come over and stay the night at my house. "It's nice to have some company," I told him before I turned in, "but really, you and Susanne are making too much of this."

I awoke to see Tom hovering over me. "Mom, what's wrong?"

"What do you mean?" I sat up. that's when I realized I was on the floor.

"You fell out of bed," Tom said. "That's the second time tonight."

"It is?" How could I have fallen from my bed and have no memory of it whatsoever? Now I was getting scared.

I didn't put up much of a fight when Tom and Susanne insisted on taking me to the emergency room. A doctor examined me and told me it was a case of the flu. I was released with instructions to take it easy.

Almost as soon as I got home, my other daughter, Nancy, phoned from Albuquerque, New Mexico. "Susanne told me what happened." Nancy quizzed me about my symptoms. "I'm going to talk to a friend who's a neurosurgeon," she said.

Within hours Nancy called again. "Mom, you should never have been released from the hospital. Pack a bag. You're coming here for tests."

"I'll never get a flight," I said. "It's Christmas Day . . ."

"No, Mom. Just sit tight. I'm coming to Colorado to get you."

Nancy drove 450 miles to pick me up, then turned right around and took me back to Albuquerque, to the hospital where her friend worked. A medical team was waiting. Tests showed my carotid artery, which supplies blood to the brain, was 95 percent blocked. That was the reason for my dizziness. I'd suffered a series of ministrokes.

"Pat, you need surgery to clear the artery," Dr. Jacobs said. "But it's risky, and I can't guarantee you'll be one hundred percent afterward. You might not be. That's why it has to be your decision to go ahead with surgery. Not mine and not your kids'."

Scared? Try terrified. But without surgery, I'd almost certainly have another stroke. I couldn't risk that. I wanted more time with my three children and with my grandchildren. What had I been reminding myself Christmas Eve at the mall? That I'd been richly blessed. *Lord, you've always taken care of me,* I prayed. *I'm trusting my life to your hands—and Dr. Jacobs's—now.*

A prevailing sense of peace settled over me. There was only one place it could have come from.

I woke after surgery, feeling that same sense of peace. One look at my daughter's face and I knew everything had gone well. "Dr. Jacobs put in a stent to keep your carotid open," Nancy said. "He says you'll make a full recovery." We called Susanne and Tom in Colorado to tell them the news. They put my grandkids on to say merry Christmas. It was like having my whole family gathered in my hospital room around me. I felt a little wistful when Nancy had to leave at the end of visiting hours.

Maybe that's why I was delighted to see a handsome young man poke his head into my room the next morning. "Hello, I'm the hospital chaplain. Is this a good time for a visit?" he asked.

"Of course," I said. "Come in, Chaplain."

He pulled up a chair to my bedside. "I like to greet all the new patients—especially when I share their last name."

"You're a Ciddio?"

"Yes, I am," he said, pointing to his nametag: Walter Ciddio. "I was making a joke. I have never met anyone else named Ciddio."

"Neither have I," I said. "Where are you from?"

"I grew up here in New Mexico. My father was from Italy, though."

It can't be, I thought. Still, I felt compelled to ask, "Your father. Was his name Ralph?"

"Yes! How did you know?"

For a moment I was too moved to speak. "My late husband, John, was Ralph's cousin," I said at last. "That would make me . . ."

"My second cousin," he whispered.

Then he gently put his arms around me and held me close. My second cousin. My sole connection to my husband's side of the family, one I had so yearned for and finally attained.

A holiday that began with a brush with death ended with an incredible reaffirmation—make that two—of life and of the Lord's unceasing love for me. See why I think Christmas is full of surprises? The best kind. Miracles.

Tahira

ZARETTE BEARD

She stood by the back doors each night as we all left the office. Every evening she was there, standing behind her giant trash can, waiting to clean up after us. I saw her watch us night after night absorbed in meaningless conversations walk right past her, as though she were invisible. She tried to make eye contact several times, but few even bothered to glance her way, much less acknowledge her presence. A smile would have been out of the question.

This irked me. I mean really irked me; so I decided I would engage this lady in a conversation. I would soon learn how difficult it was, as she had come over from Bosnia with her daughter. Her name was Tahira, and though her age was fairly young, her face and eyes revealed a sadness and a loss of innocence. It was worn several years beyond what should have been. Youth and beauty had been stolen and replaced with age and fatigue. Her English was really rough, so we usually just said a few words and used a lot of hand gestures. It was good enough.

We soon looked for one another each evening, just to say a few words to each other. Over the course of time, I learned that her husband and son were both killed in the war. She was out of options, so she came to America to work two jobs as a cleaning lady. I marveled at her courage and tenacity.

Tahira liked my Victorian office cubbie. I had draped anything that moved in purple velvet and accented my desk with antique silver picture frames, silver clocks, silver anything. We would sit in the purple cubbie and try to figure out what each other was saying over candy bars. It really was great fun.

Christmas was coming and I had decided to do something nice for Tahira. I wanted to bless her somehow, but I was afraid of embarrassing her or hurting her pride, so I came up with an idea: I secretly bought her a gift card, typed a note that said our department selected and rewarded an excellent employee each year and that she was it. I anonymously taped it to the ladies' restroom mirror for her to find. Or so I thought.

A year later, I left that company. My friend still

worked there and was surprised when Tahira frantically approached him looking for me. In her best English, she asked him to be sure I got this gift from her. He assured her he would.

There are no words to describe what happened next. I unwrapped this beautiful purple wrapping paper to find an antique glass purple bowl, a giant candy bar, and small box. I opened the box to find a silver locket with a purple flower etched on it with the words, "Forever in my heart." This amazingly thoughtful, expensive gift I received from a woman who worked two jobs and was known to me only by her first name.

I cannot tell you what Tahira's gift means to me still. Never in all of my life have I been the recipient of such a sacrificial, heartfelt gift. The bowl sits on my new desk as a constant reminder that all people have great worth. The necklace dangles close to my heart, and when I hold that precious locket in my fingers, I think of the friend I almost didn't make, Tahira. Because of her, I will never again pass a stranger without looking them in the eye and smiling.

The Christmas Thief

JACKIE CLEMENTS-MARENDA

$\mathcal{T}$hank God you weren't there when it happened." Our mother's hands folded over the telephone receiver. "You might have been injured, or worse."

My brother, Thomas, and I exchanged worried glances. It was just past 9:00 PM on Christmas Eve 1962, and we were waiting for our dad to come home for the Christmas holiday. Company downsizing had eliminated his long-held local job, and at fifty-two years old, Dad had been forced by financial circumstances to take a position with a firm located two hours away by car. Dad wouldn't consider relocating his family. With the job market so uncertain, he wasn't even sure if he would have this current job within a year. He felt that it was best for the family to stay in our familiar Brooklyn neighborhood.

The commute was hard on Dad, and he and Mom decided that he'd only come home on weekends and major holidays. Friday nights became a time of great joy in our home, while Sunday nights were dreaded. Good-byes never got any easier.

"The children will understand," Mom said into the phone. "You just be careful."

Mom hung up and took a deep breath before turning to face us. Before she even said a word, Thomas and I sensed that the news wasn't good.

"That was Dad. His car was stolen, and he's stranded in the town where he works. You both know that without a car Dad needs to take a bus and then three different trains. Since it's already so late, and since some of the depot locations are so desolate, Dad thinks it's best if he waits until tomorrow before attempting the trip."

We understood, but tears sprang to my eyes. I was nine years old, and this was the first year I was considered mature enough to attend midnight Mass with my family. Thomas, at eleven years old, was a midnight Mass veteran, and his tales of the grand celebration made me even more eager to attend. But without Dad in our pew, I knew my first midnight Mass experience would be sadly lacking.

"That's not all." The tensing of Mom's jaw betrayed the feelings she was trying to hide. "You know how much

Dad hates having to be away from us all. So this year, in order to feel like he was still very much a part of our lives, he decided to do all the Christmas shopping."

"Dad must have liked that," Thomas pointed out. "Instead of just sitting in his room at the boarding house every night after work, he had something fun to do."

"Dad had everything wrapped, ready to be placed beneath the tree as soon as he got home." Mom's brows drew together in an agonized expression. "He packed them in the trunk of the car this morning so he could leave for home right from work."

Thomas said the words she couldn't. "But the car was stolen, and all the packages were in it."

"Yes," Mom said as she flicked an imaginary speck of dust from her dress, fighting to keep her fragile control. "Even if the stores were still open, there isn't any money to replace what was lost."

A tumble of confused thoughts and feelings assailed me, and I faltered in the silence that engulfed the room. Thomas and I knew Dad had taken a large pay cut, which had meant sacrifices for all of us. Our Christmas tree was much smaller than in other years, and we were having turkey for Christmas dinner instead of the more costly roast beef. Even our Christmas wish list had contained just a few items. Had Dad gotten the miniature race car for Thomas and the golden-haired Barbie for me? How about the warm bathrobe Mom desperately needed?

"I hate the man who robbed our car!" The words burst from my lips. "He took Christmas away from us and I wish . . . I wish the man would die!"

"Jacquelyn Maria Bernadette Clements! Such a terrible thing for you to say!" Mom glared at me, frowning. "What the man did was wrong, but you must pity him. Lord knows what sort of desperate situation he's in that it drove him to steal, especially on Christmas Eve."

My eyes met Mom's disparagingly, and my lower lip trembled. I wanted to scream at her about our lost car and presents, but my brother's hand on my arm silenced me. He was right. What good would it do?

"When you're in church tonight, Jacquelyn, I think you should thank God for what we do have." Mom spoke quietly but firmly. "Sometimes the most important things in life are those you can't hold in your hand."

I'd lost interest in attending midnight Mass, but at 11:30 PM Mom helped us bundle up for the four-block walk. I had never been out at that hour. The sound of ice crunching underfoot was a counterpoint to the still night and the black sky, which was illuminated by the high, white moon and a multitude of bright stars.

Our church interior was all my brother had claimed it

would be. The bright moon allowed the arched stained glass windows to flood the house of worship with brilliant light. Ornate candles and flowers filled the altar, while parishioners who were dressed to portray various biblical characters took their places around the stable replica. Even the choir was brightly attired, ready to sing in celebration of our Lord's birth.

While Father Quinn said the Mass, I struggled to find something to be thankful for. We had no money, no car, no Christmas. I couldn't recall the last time Thomas and I went to a Saturday matinee with our friends, and Mom didn't even bake our favorite chocolate chip cookies anymore. Food necessities, such as milk and bread, came first, and there was rarely any money left over for sweets of any kind. Even our yearly summer visit to our grandparents' was doubtful with bus fares being what they were.

The sudden cry of the baby portraying the Christ child drew my attention to the stable scene. But my eyes traveled past the infant, lovingly held in the arms of the Mother Mary actress, and came to rest on a figure who had just entered through the side church door. It was Dad!

A joy I had never known swelled up within me, lifting with it all the shadows that darkened my young heart. I poked Thomas and pointed; he did the same to Mom.

Our already crowded pew mates slid over a bit more so Dad could squeeze in with us. Our family clasped hands, and I realized I had found something to be thankful for: despite all odds, Dad was home with us for Christmas.

"It was more than a coincidence—it was divine intervention," Dad later explained. "A truck driver in the phone booth next to mine overheard my conversation, and he insisted on helping me get home. He used his radio to contact other drivers along the way, and at rest stops I was passed from one truck to another. Each driver took me as far as he could. The last one dropped me off right in front of the church."

The kindness of strangers on a cold winter's night was another thing for me to be thankful for. The third blessing arrived on Christmas Day when our car was found abandoned about one hundred miles from where it had been stolen. There was minor front-end damage but, surprisingly, the trunk was never opened. All our Christmas gifts were safe.

Only hours before, this fact would have mattered more to me than anything else. However, it provided a mere jump on my happiness scale as I sat playing Monopoly with Dad.

How right Mom had been when she told me,

"Sometimes the most important things in life are those you can't hold in your hand." The spirit of Christmas dwells within our hearts, and no one, not even the most skilled thief, can ever take it away.

A Decent Place to Live

PEARL JONES

*A*s I approached the ancient building looming against the darkening winter sky, my heart beat faster with apprehension. An icy wind off the East River whipped down Harlem's 116th Street, swirling old newspapers and dirt around my feet as I halted before the building's crumbling stone steps. I looked up at the windows; most were empty smoke-blackened frames that stared down at me like the eye sockets of a skull. I shivered.

I didn't want to enter the hall and climb those steps. But I gripped my purse tighter, sloshed through the stagnant water inside the door and then climbed flight after flight of rotten stairs. Finally I reached a battered green door on the fourth floor, knocked quickly three times and waited for the metallic clatter of many chain bolts and latches being unfastened.

The door opened and my five children swarmed around me. I was home.

"Hi, honey," called my husband, who had already started supper. As he gathered me into his arms, I broke down.

"Sam," I sobbed, "I just can't make that hall and stairs anymore."

"I know, honey," he said softly.

Sam and I had moved to New York City from Charleston, South Carolina, twelve years before. He had found work in a bookbinding firm. And now we had four daughters, ages ten to fifteen, and a son, nine.

The building hadn't been too bad when we first moved into it. But the landlord had seemingly forgotten it. As the building deteriorated, families moved out, and junkies moved into the empty rooms. Now only three families were left in the six-floor building.

When I wasn't working at my job as an aide at a local public school, I'd be out hunting a better place to live. We'd been trying for years, but finding something nice we could afford seemed impossible.

As with so many families in New York City, the housing situation for us had become a nightmare. There just weren't enough decent living places available at reasonable rents. Because of our income we qualified for public housing. But that seemed hopeless. The public-housing office said it was difficult to find a place for our size family at what we could pay, and usually we were left with, "We'll call you." They never seemed to call, and I was weary of the red tape, the countless letters I had to write, the hours of waiting in housing offices.

In the meantime, I tried to find a place on my own. I searched the classified ads. One ad in the *Amsterdam News* led me up six flights to a place with crumbling walls. In another, the superintendent's wife was screaming and swearing so that I knew it was no place for us. Once I gave a man a $125 deposit on a nice-looking place and never heard from him again.

Months went by. At night I'd lie awake as rats scuttled across our floors and dream of the apartment. It would be a nice clean place with four bedrooms, two for the girls, one for Sam Jr., and one for us.

But in the morning there would be the same old bathroom with the rusty pipes and splintered timbers where the wall had once stood.

One morning an explosion came from Irene and Jackie's room. Sam and I ran in to find them screaming under a pile of plaster. The ceiling had fallen down. Fortunately, they were only scratched and bruised.

It finally got so that Sam and I could never sleep at the

same time. One of us had to stay awake at night to watch and listen. No telling what could happen with junkies staying in the building.

One evening my oldest daughter and I met a man with a gun in our downstairs hall. He staggered and shuffled out the door. I was still shaking the next morning.

"What's the matter, Pearl?" asked Helen Parham. She is my good friend who works in the school office as a secretary.

I broke into sobs and told her all our troubles. "We'll just never find a place."

She comforted me. A little later that day she asked, "Do you have a Bible, Pearl?"

"No," I sighed. "I wish I did." I thought about my father who was a deacon back in Charleston. He had taught all his children to pray. But on coming to New York, Sam and I had gotten away from praying or even thinking much about the Lord. It was such a rush-rush existence here. Back in mellow Charleston with its lazy Sundays and long warm evenings, going to church and hearing Daddy preach his sermons seemed right and natural.

A few days later, Helen invited me to her apartment for dinner. As we said good-bye she handed me a package. Even under the gift wrapping I knew what it was. There's a certain feel about a Bible.

"Now when you're feeling low, Pearl," said Helen, "just give me a ring, and we'll read the Bible together."

Sam had started working nights. And during those all-alone times when the wind rattled the windows and ominous smells and noises drifted under the door, I'd call Helen and we'd read our Bibles.

"Now, Pearl, for protection let's read Isaiah 54:17."

And we would read, "No weapon that is formed against thee shall prosper" (KJV). And then we'd go to Psalms—"I will lift up mine eyes unto the hills, from whence cometh my help" (Psalm 121:1 KJV).

Back in Charleston, we girls used to laugh and giggle as we'd recite the Scriptures with the congregation. But during those nights on the phone with my friend Helen, I began to know it as His words, His promises. And as I accepted them in my heart, the strength they gave me was miraculous. It was as if the Lord Jesus Himself was there with me in that old apartment. When I told Helen that, she said, "He is, Pearl, He is."

But still I hadn't found an apartment.

One morning at school I was telling Helen that we now had to carry an umbrella when we used the bathroom because of the dripping from above.

"Pearl," she said, "have you really asked the Lord to guide you? When you get home tonight, read Exodus 23:20."

That night I read, "Behold, I send an angel before thee, to keep thee in the way and to bring thee into the place which I have prepared."

I got such a strange feeling. Right then and there I believed He would do it. "Lord," I breathed, "I will accept that place You have prepared for us." Just taking Him at His word seemed to give me new confidence. I didn't even fear walking into our hallways anymore.

Friends marveled, "How do you do it, Pearl?"

"God will protect me," I answered.

Our apartment situation still hadn't changed. It was now December and our only heat was the gas range in the kitchen. In the daytime we'd shut the other rooms off and huddle in there, keeping the window open a bit so we wouldn't get gassed.

But I had this feeling. It was so strong that I phoned Helen one Saturday. "We're going to get an apartment for Christmas," I said.

"By Christmas!" she exlaimed. "That's only two weeks from now." She was silent for a moment. "You know, it's good to be optimistic, Pearl. But please, please, don't expect too much."

Days went by and it seemed Helen was right. I'd got to expecting too much, for there was no sign of anything.

The housing office said they had a two-bedroom place. But I knew the Lord had something better for us. I figured He wouldn't give me this good feeling for nothing. In the meantime I kept my eyes and ears open.

One day a woman in our school office mentioned that she was moving into a new apartment building.

"Where?" I asked. She said it was public housing; you had to get on a waiting list. To apply you had to have your marriage license, birth certificate, and one month's rent as a deposit. She gave me the address of the agency and right after school I headed there. It was a long bus ride. When I got there the woman I was supposed to see wasn't in.

"Come back later," a man said.

I went back two more times that afternoon. Finally at 7:00 PM the woman was there. She asked for my papers, copied them, took my check, and then said I should call her in about a week. Every time I called her she was not in.

More days went by. Meanwhile, things were getting worse in our apartment. The sink wouldn't drain anymore, and we had to dump all our dish and waste water into the toilet. Christmas was only two days away. One thing was sure: it wouldn't be much of a Christmas celebration in our old apartment. Reluctantly I made arrangements for little

Sam Jr. and our youngest girl, Andrea, to stay with some friends for Christmas.

Finally I was able to reach the housing-office lady on the phone. She asked me to come in. Another long bus ride. I sat down at her desk, she checked through my papers, then looked up. "Now where is the letter I sent you?"

"Letter? I never got one."

"No?" she asked in surprise. A peculiar expression crossed her face. Then it all came out. I was really supposed to have made an application for this apartment before it was built. And the letter she mentioned was supposed to be one saying my application had been approved.

I went cold all over. I hadn't even known about this apartment a month ago. The woman looked at me with a stricken look. It was obvious that she suddenly realized that a mistake had been made in my case. I was not due to get an apartment.

Inside I prayed.

She sat there, tapping a pencil, looking at some papers. "Well," she said, "wait a minute."

She checked through some more papers. I just sat there, still praying. And then, how or why it happened I will never know. Perhaps she felt particularly sorry for me and went beyond the call of duty. Or maybe something unexpected opened up. In any case, I just like to think it was one of God's miracles.

As I sat there feeling like time was standing still, that woman pulled out a set of plans, and then looked up at me. "We'll give you apartment 6B," she said. "It has four bedrooms, two baths, a kitchen, living room, and dining area."

I sat transfixed.

"Mrs. Jones. Do you hear me?"

I cried all the way home on the bus. She had said we could move in tomorrow! When Sam and I went to look at 6B we couldn't believe it. A new building! The elevator wasn't working yet, so we climbed the stairs. I put in our key, opened the door, and looked into the clean, clean rooms. Sam and I danced around in each one, laughing and thanking the Lord.

It was late December 24 by the time we finally finished moving in. After unpacking the last box, I said, "Sam, let's get a tree."

"Oh, honey," he groaned, "you got the apartment. You can do without a tree." Just like a man.

"Sam," I said, "God gave us this much. I'm sure that He wants us to have a Christmas tree. And if we hurry, we can also go to the store and get something for the children."

He helped me on with my coat and kissed me. "You know, honey," he said, "you're a determined woman. I'm sure glad I have a wife like you."

It was the most blessed Christmas the Joneses had ever had. And under the tree that morning were five Bibles, one for each of the children.

It was Sam's idea.

CHAPTER 3

Gifts and Glory

Then a very large group of angels from heaven joined the first angel praising God and saying, "Give glory to God in heaven" (Luke 2:13–14).

We all really enjoy receiving wonderful gifts at Christmas, don't we? Sometimes we get exactly what we had hoped for. Other times we're surprised by gifts we didn't expect but that delight and thrill us. And yet, Christmas is really only about one Gift—not one wrapped in glistening paper and shiny bows under a glimmering fir tree, but one draped in bloody rags and a crown of thorns on a cross-shaped tree. It was the most priceless Gift of all time, and the glory of that Gift still enlightens our world down through the ages. Celebrate the Gift this Christmas and its never-ending glory.

You Are Loved

SUSAN FARR FAHNCKE

She sat huddled in the doorway, trying to fight off the biting December wind. With a thin coat and her leg in a cast, she seemed small and vulnerable, but I knew she must be tough—much stronger than I or most people I knew. She was the only homeless person on the streets of San Francisco who didn't ask us for money. Never, not once.

My husband and I were on a weekend getaway to a city we both loved. (He for the sourdough bread and I for the shopping.) As we got out of our cab in front of the hotel, we saw her for the first time. I liked her right off because she wasn't drinking from a mysterious brown paper bag; she wasn't aggressively asking for money as so many other homeless people were. She was reading. Hunched over her book, trying to capture the last of the winter daylight, she struggled to both keep warm and lose herself in its pages. I wondered about her the rest of the night. I wondered what got her to this place of desolation and cold, of hunger and loneliness. I tossed and turned in our warm and clean hotel bed, knowing she was outside somewhere with nothing more than one blanket and one book.

Every time we left the hotel, we would see her in a different doorway, always keeping to herself and always reading her book. She never responded to my cheerful "Hi!" and I knew she just wanted to be left alone. She had long, dark hair, deep brown eyes, and looked small and frail huddled deep in the doorways that were her shelter from the world.

On our second night, as we headed back to the hotel, my husband and I talked about the quiet homeless woman. We both wanted to do something for her, but didn't know how she would react, since she never asked for anything and seemed to want to only rely on herself. But deep in my heart, I knew I couldn't leave without at least doing something. Christmas was looming ahead in only a couple of weeks, and my heart ached for a woman who would spend it in solitude and cold, without family, without gifts.

I said a quick prayer in my heart, asking God to help me know what we could do. Before returning to our hotel, we found a department store and wandered through, looking for exactly the right gifts for our friend who had no idea who we were. We kept looking at each other and laughing at our own excitement. Warm gloves were my husband's first suggestion. We found perfect red, thick wool gloves and grinned, knowing her hands would now be warm. Being an avid nighttime reader myself, I knew the next "must" on our list was a good flashlight and extra batteries. She could read at night and chase the demons away when the dark got to be too much for a woman sleeping in a doorway in Union Square. We added a few small treats—it was Christmas after all—and then went in search of the last gift I knew I must give her. We headed for the nearest bookstore and I said another quick prayer for guidance. Buying a book for someone is really difficult, especially if you have no idea what they like to read. Almost immediately I walked right up to exactly the right book. I felt a delicious thrill as I read the author—my favorite, Maya Angelou. Her stories and poetry told of hard times, but of deep determination and strength within. She was a woman of great strength, I knew her words would reach this woman's soul and hoped they would bring her comfort during the bitter winter she was facing.

We hurried back to the hotel to put it all together and happily spotted her just outside, once again reading her book, her leg in its cast resting on her thin blanket. I tried my "Hi!" one more time and once again she ignored me. I somehow knew this would be more a gift for me than for her.

We returned to our room and quickly filled a Christmas bag with our gifts. I wrote inside the cover of the book "Merry Christmas! You are loved." And said a quick prayer that she would accept our gifts and they would in some small way be of use to her.

Hand in hand, we walked outside again, buttoning up against the wind and half ran to her spot in the doorway.

It was empty.

We looked around and could see her nowhere. With tears in my eyes, I realized we were too late. She had found better shelter or left the area entirely. We walked the streets of Union Square until it was very late, her bag clutched in my hands and a constant prayer that we would find her in my heart. We ended up back at our hotel, the bag still with us and the woman nowhere to be found. I couldn't stop the tears. Where was she? Was she hurt or freezing or scared? I couldn't stand the thought of anyone so alone and so lost in such a big city. Now all I could do for her was pray.

The rest of the weekend my husband and I searched for her. We looked in every cubbyhole, doorway and bench that she might have gone to, but we never found her. My husband had to fly out to another state for business, and I stayed on to visit with friends living nearby.

Finally, I had only a couple of hours left in the city and my determination to find her strengthened. My friend Joe picked me up and we spent our morning looking for her yet again.

"Sooz, I think she's gone." Joe was always the realist.

"One more time around the block," I pleaded. "We'll just give it one last shot and then I'll quit." I prayed very fast and very hard.

And there she was.

For the first time, I saw her talking to other people, her back to me, her long black hair cascading down her back and her leg in its cast told me I had finally found her. There was nowhere to park, and Joe quickly circled the block again. Spotting her and not wanting to lose her again, I jumped out of the car and sprinted over to the group. Suddenly I was embarrassed and feeling stupid. Well, I was here and I couldn't turn back now.

I tapped her on the shoulder, and as she turned around I grinned like a kid, held out her bag and finally got to say my "Merry Christmas!" to the woman I had agonized over and prayed about for three days.

I wasn't sure how she would react, since she seemed not interested in making friends, but what she did next brought tears and made my heart swell.

"Oh, *thank* you!" She snatched the Christmas bag and without hesitation peered inside. She stared hard and when she looked back up at me, her eyes, too, were filled with tears. "A Christmas present." She sounded as if she hadn't had a gift in a very long time. "Thank you!" she said again and my teary words are now a blur, but I reached out and hugged her tight. I then found myself saying something I had not planned on.

"I just want you to know . . . You are loved." She looked as surprised as I was, but I saw the tears and knew I had delivered my message, given the gift I was meant to. With trembling legs, I walked away, to my friend's car and away from her forever.

I'll never forget that incredible woman who braved the hardest thing I can imagine with quiet dignity and courage. I hope she is somewhere warm and safe, and I hope she knows she is loved. She never asked for a thing, but what she gave me will stay with me for a lifetime.

A Child Is Born

SUE FERGUSON

The sun hadn't risen yet on this memorable Christmas morning. Across the room tiny white lights sparkled on the tree like stars in the sky, and the small, solitary bulb protruding through the hole at the back of the rustic, wooden stable shined with announcement. My eyes rested on the figures in the stable. Mary and Joseph stood straight, their felt bodies weighted with dry kidney beans. A few simple embroidery stitches marked their faces. Jesus rested in the manger; outline stitches defined his face and swaddling clothes. Golden yarn fringed the edge of the manger, and a few strands of hay lay scattered about. A disheveled shepherd and two white sheep were in a pile next to the stable, most likely bumped when a gift was placed nearby. Wise men approached from a distance. I could see them, in the shadows behind several festively wrapped packages, wearing shimmering turbans and brightly colored sashes. They carried ornate gifts.

Randy, my husband, and I made the polyester stuffed holy family to endure our two-year-old's curious and playful hands. The wooden stable and laminated companion picture book completed our creative efforts. Deciding to put the stable under the tree, surrounded by wrapped packages, was a deliberate choice; we wanted Nathan to experience Jesus as the best gift of all.

But in the quiet darkness just before dawn that Christmas, the message was for me, not Nathan. I had a new appreciation for God's great gift and its packaging. A few days before, the bright afternoon sunshine couldn't have brightened my heart like those tiny lights and the lone stable bulb did early that morning. Wonder and delight replaced my previous apprehension. The miracle I had experienced brought new awareness and excitement to the wonder of Christmas!

That day, just eleven days before, had begun like most days during my pregnancy; I felt sick. Our second child was due in mid January. Joyful anticipation didn't eliminate the effects of fatigue and nausea; I was weary. Just like any other two-year-old, Nathan required more energy than I possessed. The house was dusty and cluttered. My usually empty sink was overflowing with dishes. Laundry piles reached to the ceiling. I was dreading Christmas.

Months earlier my mother and brother's family had graciously agreed to celebrate the holiday at our house. Instead of being grateful I wasn't traveling, I was overwhelmed. Wanting my loving family to arrive to a home sparkling with decorations and smelling delicious only magnified my feeling of chaos. We needed a miracle, but honestly, I wasn't expecting one.

The day God designed to offer joy and peace with the gift of His Son seemed destined for misery. The many activities of the season only made it worse. My husband's position as a minister kept him busy night after night with a variety of committee and office parties. Normally he would have come home from work to lend his hands, but he was also tired and weary. I couldn't tell my family not to come; the thought of not sharing the holiday was worse. They would help when they arrived, and we would make the best of the situation. If only I felt good enough to catch up on a few routine tasks!

Finally I reached my limit. Randy arrived home at ten o'clock one evening. "We just can't go on like this," I whimpered between sobs. Since my mother-in-law wasn't employed, I pleaded, "Call your mom and see if she can come for a few days, please." He agreed and immediately dialed for help.

Of course Randy's mom was busy getting ready for her own holiday celebration, but knowing a request meant we were desperate, she made plans to make the long, familiar drive. My relief was instant, but I still felt guilty. My tired husband was cramming clothes into the washer and unloading the dishwasher, only to load it again. He needed rest too. And I felt sick, really sick.

My back ached; I didn't want to move. Each time Randy passed through the bedroom as he tended to the dishes and laundry (fortunately our two-year-old was asleep), I begged him to rub my back. He accommodated me briefly and then went back to the household tasks. There was no reprieve from my back pain. In a recent childbirth class we'd been told to get down on all fours, like you're going to crawl, and slowly raise and lower your back like a cat for back pain. I crept to the floor to experiment, anxious for some relief. As soon as I raised my back, a shot of pain went through my body, and I let out a scream. My husband rushed to my side to remind me to be quiet; he didn't want Nathan to wake up. He sure didn't need anyone or anything else to take care of that night. Or did he?

As my weary husband helped me back into bed, my water broke. Without hesitation, the childbirth training kicked in, and he was transformed into a model labor coach. "It's going to be okay. I'll call the neighbors to come get Nathan, and we'll go to the hospital."

"There's not time."

He soon realized, too, that our baby was coming quickly! "I'll call an ambulance."

"There's not time!"

Before the ambulance could arrive, my husband, like Mary's Joseph, attended to his wife, and a child was born. Jesus was born in a stable because there was no room in the inn. Our daughter Karissa was born in our little house because there was no time to get to the hospital. Angels sang the glorious announcement of Jesus' birth. Randy used the telephone to tell surprised family members and friends our baby had arrived five weeks early.

Shepherds and sheep were Jesus' first guests. Our home welcomed a pair of overly enthusiastic volunteer paramedics. I cringed as one of them bounced into my bedroom carrying a disposable obstetrical kit cheering, "My first baby, my first baby!"

Moved from the bed to a hard, straight stretcher, my baby and I were carried down the stairs and out the door to a waiting ambulance. Our ride to the hospital was bumpy and uncomfortable, but brief and joy-filled. Mary had to travel slowly for miles, on a donkey, while still anxiously anticipating the birth of her son. Wise men brought gold, frankincense, and myrrh to Jesus; our friends delivered casseroles, holiday treats, and pink-bowed packages to us.

On that unforgettable Christmas morning I sat in my rocker and pondered the wonder of the past twelve days. I felt great. All the chaos was gone. My family had arrived safely. The house was in order, the kitchen was filled with edible delights, and everyone was still sleeping. Well everyone but me; I was holding a peaceful baby. Karissa had just finished an early morning feeding. I gazed into the stable under the twinkling tree, too excited to sleep. Everyone would be up in a few hours and the gifts surrounding the tree would be opened. None would compare to the best gift of all, the one aglow in that wooden stable lying in the manger.

My baby arrived, as Jesus did, totally dependent on a young woman and her husband for care. God sacrificially chose to lower Himself into my human world so I might be lifted up to know Him. The glory of it all was just too much to grasp! God chose for His Son to become human, as human as my baby, and yet be divine . . . what a gift, what a miracle!

Jeffrey's Gift

DONNA LOWICH

*I*t's Christmas 1986. The Christmas tree is resplendent in its ornaments and lights; they blink on and off with their reflection glittering in the beautifully wrapped gifts below the tree. Five-year-old Jeffrey is dancing around the tree, singing, "The Christmas tree is *sooo* much bigger than last year!" always emphasizing the "*soo.*"

I enjoyed watching him having fun. His enthusiasm and excitement were really something to behold! Jeffrey turned to me, his huge chocolate-brown eyes brimming with excitement and shining with happiness. "Isn't the tree beautiful and much bigger than last year's tree, Mommy?"

True enough, it was a big, beautiful tree. And it was a much bigger tree than last year's tree. Or at least that's what I've been told.

Christmas 1985 is not even a memory for me. I had just undergone two spinal cord surgeries. I was paralyzed from the shoulders down, and due to other complications, I don't have any recollection of that holiday. My husband, Walter, knew that Jeffrey needed to have Christmas, but all he could manage was a table-top tree. He tried to make it festive, but it was very difficult for both of them. Hence, Jeffrey's exuberance this year. I was home, and we were going to have a festive Christmas. No wonder the tree seemed so big.

I, too, was so happy to be home! After all, that had been my main focus for the six months I had been in the hospital and then in the rehab center. But I always had it in mind that when I came home everything would be as it used to be. But it wasn't, and that bothered me. I was disappointed in myself because, while I was still making progress, it was slow, and I was not nearly where I had expected to be in my recovery. It was not anger so much as it was frustration with myself.

With these thoughts in mind, I got up slowly from my chair and made my way to the stairs. Jeffrey stopped singing and I knew he was watching me as I struggled to climb the stairs. I heard quick little running steps. I turned, and he was there, right there next to me. He was always there when I needed him.

He held my hand. Looking directly at me, he said, "Sometimes I wish it was me."

Gripped by the power of his words, I hugged him tightly, burying my face in his wavy brown hair, squeezing my eyes shut to fight back the tears.

"Oh no, Jeffrey, no!" is all I could manage before he began to speak again.

"That way, you could carry me up the stairs." Now his eyes were brimming with tears. He looked down at the floor, saying, "I can't carry you."

Those words of love, a child's love, so symbolic of the season, jolted me like nothing else could. In an instant, it changed everything for me—from melancholy to a deep sense of gratitude, love, and peace. No, things were not the same as they once were, but now I realized just how unimportant that truly was. To this day, when my frustrations get the better of me (as they sometimes do) my thoughts go back to that moment in time when my five-year-old son taught me a very powerful and poignant lesson. Nothing like a little role reversal to keep one's priorities straight!

I spoke to Jeffrey with the only words I could find to say, "No matter what, Jeffrey, I will always be your Mommy, and I will always be here for you, no matter what. I love you, Jeffrey. Merry Christmas, my little professor."

He was my professor, you see, for he was continually teaching me life's important lessons. He looked up at me and smiled. While I was frustrated with my lot in life, he saw through all that and was happy just to have me home again. Simple and straightforward—the truth always is— it sometimes takes a child to pinpoint it with such uncanny accuracy.

I looked over at the Christmas tree. It had assumed a new aura of the warmth, the peace, and the beauty the Christmas season brings to us. It absolutely glowed with love—love of family, love of life itself. It was there all the time; I just needed the love and selflessness of a five-year-old boy to teach me that lesson.

Jeffrey had just taught me that it wasn't important that I couldn't walk very far or do things quite as I used to. It was important that I had been given the chance to be home with my family at Christmas. I was given so much more than was ever taken away. I now knew that. And that is Jeffrey's gift, the sweetest gift of all, wrapped in the beauty of a little boy's unconditional, forgiving love.

Thank you, Jeffrey. Merry Christmas, my little professor.

The Watch

ZARETTE BEARD

My son, Sabian is a *Star Wars* fan. Okay, not just a fan, a fanatic. The kid lives and breathes *Star Wars,* which is pretty normal for a twelve-year-old, or so I'm told. I wanted to get him something really special for Christmas, and nothing was really grabbing my attention until I saw the watch.

It was in a spinning case. I squeezed through the people waiting at the counter and slowly spun the case around to see if what I thought I saw was really there. It was. There in that case was the manliest, chunky, silver men's watch I'd ever seen. Darth Vader was blanketed in silver and stared menacingly back at me through the case. I had to have it. I looked side to side to see if anyone else had seen it. I motioned for the sales clerk to open the case, and I grabbed it before anyone else could. It was perfect.

Christmas morning, Sabian opened the gift, and his

expression verified what I already knew. I gently warned him about caring for the watch. He wore it proudly for the next few days, but I noticed he kept taking it off. I warned him again that he would lose it if he kept taking it off.

We were at the grocery store when my son had excused himself to wash his hands. I started to wonder where he was when he approached, head hung, and his face stained with tears. His mouth was stuck open and he looked like he was in shock, which sent me into an immediate panic. I ran to him, demanding to know what happened. He managed to choke out that he had taken his watch off to wash his hands and it was gone. We alerted the store manager, and my husband and I began a frantic search. I left my name and phone number with the manager, knowing it wouldn't matter. The watch was gone. My son was inconsolable, and I thought I would be sick.

I didn't have the heart, or stomach for that matter, for an "I told you so." I just kept quiet and ached for my son. I thought it might be a good time for a light lesson about turning in things that you find, because they belong to someone, and that someone is missing that thing. Sabian made the comment that someone got a really great watch that night. With an ounce of faith and a pound of cynicism, I prayed with my son that whoever found the watch would turn it in. Then he said something that dropped my jaw to the floor; he said that he hoped that whoever took it would get a lot of joy from it. I secretly was hoping they'd break out with a bad case of leprosy, thus showing my vengeful attitude.

We got home and I sent him to bed. Feeling completely defeated, I picked up the phone to see if there were any messages. There was one. I dialed the number, and again my mouth fell open; it was the store clerk. Someone had turned in the watch, and the clerk had called to tell me they would hold it for me.

I am so grateful that prayers are answered by love, not by the faith of a cynical mom.

Christmas Smiles

SUSAN FARR FAHNCKE

For some reason, this time of year seems to bring out the grumpy in people. The day after Thanksgiving, I was up at 4:00 AM, shopping with all the other crazy people, and still, I held on to my holiday cheer and my smile. I felt sorry for the people with scowls on their faces, short-tempered with store clerks, shoppers, and other holiday drivers. They were missing all the fun, the joy in gathering gifts for loved ones.

However, with each passing day, my to-do list grew, and I fell more and more behind. I was soon feeling overwhelmed, drowning actually, in all that needed to be done. I found myself growing more irritable every day. I knew my face looked every bit as cranky and negative about the hustle and bustle as those I had been pitying earlier.

My stacks of cards, waiting to be signed and sent, my lists of baking to be done, the gifts that I could never quite

115

get finished, all beckoned one very tired mother. Work got behind, my house suffered the in-between Thanksgiving and Christmas décor, and soon the spirit of Christmas was only found in brief sporadic moments when my heart opened up enough to let it in.

Soon Christmas cards poured in, more than I had ever seen in one year, and although they made me feel loved, they also reminded me of all that I still had to do.

I plowed through the to-do list, not with my usual enthusiasm and sense of joy, but with a sense of "hurry up and get it done," something to cross off the list so I felt that I had accomplished something, anything. I knew my sense of gloom was stemming from pregnancy, constant fatigue, and early contractions, added to caring for three children, three jobs, a house to run, two holiday-time birthdays in our home, just more than ever to do and less energy to do it with. But I really wanted to feel the Christmas spirit I usually did. I wanted this time to be magical for my children, not for them to feel my stress and let it ruin such a wonderful time for them.

My nightly prayers quickly became nothing more than a simple plea for me to overcome this perpetual cranki-ness, followed by my falling asleep before I even got to "Amen." The knowledge of this, too, added to my sense of always falling behind.

Shopping with my youngest son this week brought the simplest solution, one that had never occurred to me and yet was the exact healing my spirit needed.

Starting off with my list of Christmas shopping still needing to be finished and Christmas looming only a few days away, I could feel the rest of the to-do list still nagging the back of my brain. I left the house without my smile and the beginnings of grumpy sneaking in already. My little Noah, who has never felt a bad mood in his life, skipped ahead of me, his energy and love for life apparent in all that he does.

I headed onto the freeway, and immediately the car in the lane I was merging into sped up, trying to get past me before I could get on the freeway. Irritated, I veered to the shoulder, slowing down, and waiting for room to merge back in. The car suddenly moved over to the next lane, giving me the room I needed. Surprised, I glanced over at the driver, and was even more surprised to see him smile broadly and wave. Belatedly, I smiled back, and no one saw it but Noah in the backseat.

"Why are you smiling?" Noah asked me in sign language. Being deaf, he watches my face closely at all times.

Embarrassed and angry at myself, I realized how seldom I must be smiling for my little guy to ask me *why* I am doing it now. I told him I was smiling because he makes me happy. A tiny white lie, but by now this was the true reason for my smile.

Next stop was the off-ramp and the mall exit. Always crowded, I knew today would be worse than normal. I pulled off and waited in the long line to get off the exit ramp. I happened to glance over at the same time the man in the car next to me happened to glance at me. Instead of the scowl I usually saw on my fellow drivers' faces, this man shot me a smile, warm and genuine. I instantly felt my own smile spread across my face and grinned right back at him. Wow, two complete strangers in the middle of holiday traffic, being kind and friendly. What do you know!

I found my smile more at the ready and myself more willing to pass it on. I was surprised at how much better it made my day, how it also seemed to change others' stressed-out holiday faces into cheerful Christmas smiles. Funny how it works that way. Good or bad moods have a way of creating the ripple effect.

On the way home from our errands, I caught great big grins in a car load of ladies' faces. I smiled back and reflected how happy everyone seemed all of a sudden. Day after day I have been seeing cranky, tired, stressed-out people, trying to catch up with Christmas, myself included, and all of a sudden the world seems happy, almost joyful. We passed another car and a little girl waved and smiled, her mother laughing with holiday cheer.

Wondering at this happy epidemic, I happened to glance in my rear view mirror and catch a glimpse of a red Santa hat, and a tiny little waving hand coming from my backseat.

Cranking my mirror down lower, I caught the culprit. Noah sat happily, Santa hat, grin, and wave at the ready, passing on Christmas cheer to anyone who would look. Having that dimpled, truly joyful grin directed at me, I wondered at how I could ever live a day without bubbling over in gratitude.

Laughing at my little miracle maker, I wondered how many people had been affected by his smile and contagious grin. How many people found themselves smiling at their families tonight, or the store clerks and other drivers, all because the little boy in the Santa hat smiled at them? The power of one wee little smile can create more change than all the Christmas presents in the world.

I drove home, resolving to savor this feeling and let Noah's smile stay in my heart, and hoping I was not the only one whose Christmas smile was found again.

Bound by Love

KRISTI DENTON

*I*t was ten days before Christmas 1995, and I could hardly wait! David and I had hung every tree, every bush, every roof edge and porch line on our little house in Cookeville, Tennessee, with colored bulbs—twelve hundred of them.

I switched on the strings one by one and stood in the doorway, listening for David's motorcycle. Any minute he'd be home from his sales job at the lumber mill. With my secretary's salary on top of his, we'd agreed to splurge for Christmas. I pictured David's face when he saw his present, hidden for the moment in my parents' basement. December 26 would be our third anniversary; for his combined gift I'd bought a table saw and router for his woodworking.

It was after 5:00 PM—where was he? He'd promised to get home early. My office Christmas party was at 6:00 PM, and we both had to get ready. "We've got to be on time," I'd reminded him. "I'm bringing the food."

"I won't be late," he'd said.

I took a shower, and David still wasn't back. Probably got held up by friends, I grumbled. David had a lot of friends. I could never just walk up to a stranger and start talking as he could. He was probably having fun somewhere and had forgotten all about the time.

By 5:45 PM I was frantic. It was unthinkable that I might go without him. *Don't start yelling when he walks in,* I told myself. We'd been at each other lately, both of us working too hard and not spending as much time together. *Think of all the things you love about him.*

That was easy. I had worshiped David ever since we were in a typing class together in high school: me a lowly sophomore; David a handsome senior, a star on the baseball team. I couldn't believe it when he invited me water skiing that summer. We dated for five years, till he finished at Tennessee Tech—David wouldn't get married until he could support me.

Even with a degree, though, he couldn't find work in the small town of Moss, Tennessee, where we'd both grown up. I'd cried for days when we moved to Cookeville.

It's only an hour from Moss, but to me it might as well have been the moon. I was a mama's girl who'd never lived among people I didn't know. The first six months in Cookeville I'd been so miserable that only David's love kept me from running home to Moss. He knew how I depended on him, which made his letting me down the night of my Christmas party that much worse. By 6:00 PM I was nearly in tears.

Then the phone rang. There'd been an accident. A dump truck had turned directly into the path of David's motorcycle. David was being airlifted to Erlanger Medical Center in Chattanooga because of a leg injury.

All through the dark two-hour drive to Chattanooga I wondered how I'd manage if David were laid up in the hospital while his leg healed. I'd never been on my own even for a day. At Erlanger they wouldn't let me see him. I couldn't understand why. The family started gathering in the waiting room. For the first time it occurred to me they wouldn't airlift someone who had only broken a leg.

At last a doctor appeared. "It's bad news. The brain stem was sheared. He might live twelve hours. I'm sorry."

People were crying, hugging me, holding one another. And I heard myself say in a tone so strong it surprised everyone, "David's not going to die. God is going to give us a miracle."

Friends and relatives kept coming. When twelve hours passed and David was still alive, doctors gave him twenty-four hours. Then forty-eight. We took turns around the clock in the hospital's prayer room.

It was hard to keep believing in a miracle when I was finally allowed into the trauma unit. David lay in a coma, and machines were doing the work of his body. Doctors said they could keep him technically alive, but he'd never regain consciousness. Could I stay strong for David, for myself, strong as the words I'd spoken when I declared God would grant us a miracle?

I tried to close my ears against the doctors' words, tried to picture David opening his eyes, sitting up, spreading his arms to take me in them. His mother found a verse in Isaiah that we claimed as a promise: "They that wait upon the LORD shall renew their strength; they shall mount up with wings as eagles" (40:31 KJV). That very day the mail brought a get-well card with a picture of a soaring eagle. I propped the card on the monitor attached to David's skull.

To combat David's grim prognosis, we decorated his

room with tokens of hope. We plastered the walls with cards, played music, talked to him as though he were awake.

I'd never been close to David's parents because I felt intimidated by them. But that didn't seem to matter now. Nothing mattered except praying for David.

On Christmas morning, ten days after the accident, there was a small change in the motionless form on the bed: David's eyelids opened a tiny, tiny slit. Nurses dismissed the event as a reflex, but I knew it was my Christmas gift from God.

By New Year's Day, although he didn't appear to be seeing, David's eyes had opened wider. The day his mother and I left the hospital for the first time, there was another gift. For more than two weeks we'd been sleeping on chairs in the waiting room, washing at the basin in the ladies' room. As word of our situation got around, church people in Chattanooga opened their homes to us. As we left for our first real shower, a rainbow stretched from one end of the sky to the other.

One month after the accident, breathing on his own, David was transferred from the hospital trauma unit to the Siskin Hospital for Physical Rehabilitation next door. Here I learned to turn him in bed, clear his trachea tube, change his diapers. Therapists gradually raised him to a sitting position, then to standing. With five of us supporting him—a nurse under each arm, his mother and I each at a leg, his father holding his head—we put David through the motions of walking day after day.

Still there was no way to tell what, if anything, David was aware of. He was definitely seeing, though, following us with his eyes. His fourth month at Siskin, he began making sounds, a meaningless babble at first, but I thought, *He's trying to communicate.* At last, one day as his sister was feeding him, came the moment I'll never forget.

David's lips parted, and three syllables came from his mouth . . . slow, halting, but unmistakable: "Had enough."

Somewhere inside that broken body, the David I knew and loved was very much alive, strong minded, and independent as ever.

In July, seven months after the accident, with a railed bed set up in our house in Cookeville and family to help me, we moved him home. Colored lights still festooned the yard. As I took them down, I promised myself that in December we'd make up for the Christmas we'd missed.

I clung desperately to that thought when 1996 came to an end, and the Christmas I was waiting for hadn't happened. For though David continued to confound medical experts, the brain injury had affected his memory. As his speech therapist helped him form more words, it became clear that he'd lost the previous ten years of his life. It was 1997 on the calendar; for David it was 1987. He recognized his parents, his sisters, boyhood friends, but when he looked at me I saw only puzzlement in his eyes. Who was this stranger who never left his side? When he called me "that girl" I'd go out on our porch and cry. "Lord," I prayed, "let him remember how much we love each other." But as David regained some control over his muscles, he'd tug at the gold band on his ring finger. As far as he knew, he was still in high school. Why was he wearing a wedding ring?

By April 1997 David had advanced enough to enter the Bill Wilkerson Center in Nashville. Again strangers from local churches opened their homes to me and the rest of the family. Throughout his six months there, pieces of the missing years would suddenly fall into place for David, often to be lost again the next day. But he was making progress—slow, not always steady, little by little renewing his strength as Isaiah promised.

One morning as I helped him navigate a corridor with his walker, he turned to me. "We . . . went water skiing," he said. I looked at him, agog. "Our . . . first date," he continued, as if trying to jog my memory.

"Oh, David," I whispered, "of course I remember!"

Another big step forward was his getting a job assembling shipping boxes, part of a state program for the disabled. I knew how much earning a wage, however small, meant to his proudly independent spirit.

Finances were a constant struggle—payments on the house, the car—especially for me. David had always managed that side of things. But our families helped out, and eventually there was a settlement from the company that owned the dump truck.

Through it all, I kept seeing the effect David had on everyone who came into contact with him. Doctors, therapists, patients, visitors, all were uplifted by his pluck, his faith, his good humor. One nurse told me, "Your husband has such a wonderful smile! When I'm tired I just have to step into his room, and I can keep going."

It was not until October 1997, almost two years after the accident, that David and I returned for good to our little house in Cookeville. It was the moment I'd dreamed of, the two of us alone together at last, picking up right where we'd left off.

Reality was different. As the only one with him, I was also the sole outlet for David's frustration. He was back among familiar things, yet nothing was the same. A fishing pole he couldn't use, a pickup he couldn't drive, photographs of events he couldn't remember. I still had to watch him constantly, lift him after his frequent falls, care for the house, balance the budget—and if this was hard on me, it was agony for David.

Sometimes it was easier to speak to each other through Ricco, a West Highland white terrier we had bought. "Ricco, tell David it's time for his bath." "Ricco, tell Kristi I want to lie down."

Christmas 1997 came, the third one after the accident, and the table saw and router remained in my parents' basement. David had planned to surprise me that Christmas in 1995, too, I'd discovered; I found a gray velvet jewelry box hidden under his bedside table. I put it in our safe-deposit box without peeking.

The New Year arrived, 1998, and David's stubborn courage kept gaining small victories. Though he still saw double images, his balance improved, and he graduated from a walker to a quad cane. By that summer, however, it was clear to us both that he would not return to his job at the lumber mill. We would be better off in Moss, near our families.

We left Cookeville a week before Christmas 1998. The twelve hundred colored bulbs were packed away for the move, but before we left, we had that long-postponed celebration. I didn't give David the tools. It had taken me three years to accept the changes in our lives and give up the scenario I'd held on to.

Still, it was a wonderful Christmas party. Sears let me exchange the table saw and router for a three-wheeled bicycle with a basket in which David could carry Ricco and his cane. Inside the gray velvet box was a diamond wrap to wear around my wedding ring, as a token of our love that keeps growing stronger.

"They shall renew their strength," Isaiah promises, and that is what's happening, every day. David's physical recovery is part of it, but there's so much more. I'd overlooked the all-important word in that verse: *wait.*

I thought waiting on the Lord meant marking time till healing came. I've learned that it's the wait itself that creates the healing—far beyond anything we ask. I think of the scores of people who, like that nurse at the Bill Wilkerson Center, have had their own breakthroughs because of meeting David.

I think of myself, how I was wary of strangers, and how strangers housed and cared for me month after month and became friends. I think of how hard it had been to read the Bible, and how truth and joy leap from its pages for me now. How I'd never been close to David's folks, and how we're now one family, the happiest one I know. How I used to say "I can't," and now I know I can.

We've had that miracle, all right. Not the one of my fantasy. My husband didn't wake from his coma restored in an instant. I know now that God's miracles usually happen over time. Waiting on the Lord means walking in His company step by single step, while He shows us how much He loves us.

David and I are renting a small place in Moss, while, with the help of our families, we build our dream house, a rustic log home with a view of distant hills. Our goal is to move in this Christmas 1999. We'd like to string those colored lights out to welcome the year 2000.

But if the house isn't ready by then, we can wait.

Undelivered Gifts

WAYNE MONTGOMERY

*H*ave you ever had the experience of almost not doing an act of thoughtfulness or charity—only to discover later that without this action on your part a very important experience would not have happened to someone else?

Whenever I am tempted to be lazy or indifferent in this way, I inevitably think back to that Christmas in Korea in 1951.

It was late afternoon on December 24. After a cold, miserable ride by truck in the snow, I was back at our command post. Shedding wet clothing, I relaxed on a cot and dozed off. A young soldier came in and in my sleep-fogged condition I heard him say to the clerk, "I wish I could talk to the sergeant about this."

"Go ahead," I mumbled, "I'm not asleep."

The soldier then told me about a group of Korean civilians four miles to the north who had been forced to leave their burning village. The group included one woman ready to give birth. His information had come from a Korean boy who said these people badly needed help.

My first inner reaction was, *How could we ever find the refugees in this snow?* Besides, I was dead tired. Yet something told me we should try.

"Go get Crall, Pringle, and Graff," I said to the clerk. When these soldiers arrived, I told them my plan, and they agreed to accompany me. We gathered together some food and blankets; then I saw the box of Christmas packages in the corner of the office. They were presents sent over from charity organizations in the States. We collected an armful of packages and started out by jeep.

After driving several miles, the snow became so blinding that we decided to approach the village by foot. After what seemed like hours, we came to an abandoned mission.

The roof was gone, but the walls were intact. We built a fire in the fireplace, wondering what to do next. Graff opened one of the Christmas packages in which he found some small, artificial Christmas trees and candles. These he placed on the mantel of the fireplace.

I knew it made no sense to go on in this blizzard. We finally decided to leave the food, blankets, and presents there in the mission in the hope that some needy people would find them. Then we groped our way back to the command post.

In April 1952 I was wounded in action and taken to the hospital at Won Ju. One afternoon while basking in the sun, a Korean boy joined me. He was a talkative lad and I only half listened as he rambled on.

Then he began to tell me a story that literally made me jump from my chair. After he finished, I took the boy to our chaplain; he helped me find an elder of the local Korean church who verified the boy's story.

"Yes, it was a true miracle—an act of God," the Korean churchman said. Then he told how on the previous Christmas Eve he was one of a group of Korean civilians who had been wandering about the countryside for days after North Korean soldiers had burned their village. They were nearly starved when they arrived at an old mission. A pregnant woman in their group was in desperate condition.

"As we approached the mission, we saw smoke coming from the chimney," the Korean said. "We feared that North Korean soldiers were there but decided to go in anyway. To our relief, the mission was empty. But, lo and behold, there were candles on the mantel, along with little trees! There were blankets and boxes of food and presents! It was a miracle!"

The old man's eyes filled with tears as he described how they all got down on their knees and thanked God for their deliverance. They made a bed for the pregnant woman and built a little shelter over her. There was plenty of wood to burn and food to eat and they were comfortable for the first time in weeks. It was Christmas Eve.

"The baby was born on Christmas Day," the man said. He paused. "The situation couldn't have been too different from that other birth years ago."

On the following morning, American soldiers rescued the Koreans, who later became the nucleus of a Christian church in the village where I was recuperating.

You just never know when you have a special role to play in one of God's miracles.

A Cherished Past,
A Hopeful Present

TRISTA LINMAN

Standing only two feet tall, it wasn't much of a tree. They decorated it with a popcorn strand and put a tin-foil star on top. It was all they could afford.

Neil's latest assignment had placed him and his new wife, Jan, in a foreign country with no family or friends. Nevertheless, the delight of their first year together made the spirit of Christmas more special than ever, and they relished the opportunity to reflect on the true meaning of the season.

They sat by their tree on Christmas Eve and took turns reading the story of Jesus' birth from the book Jan's parents had sent them. It was a beautiful book—definitely the most expensive item they owned. When they finished reading, they decided to exchange their gifts.

Neil picked his up first and handed it to Jan. She gently unwrapped it and found a pair of costume earrings inside. "They're beautiful," she said as she clipped them on.

Jan then proudly handed Neil his present. He opened it to reveal a knitted blue cap. Neil grinned. Looking over at Jan's knitting bag in the opposite corner of the room, he inquired, "Did you make this?"

She nodded, smiling proudly.

Neil was touched. The time and thought Jan had put into his gift made it worth much more than the price of its yarn. "You're wonderful," he whispered, leaning over to give his new wife a loving kiss.

For the next several years, Neil wore the blue cap every winter, even after they could afford nicer ones. They eventually bought a comfortable home and raised three children there. For twenty-five years, their lives together were blessed. But once the kids were grown, Jan was stricken with a serious disease. Although she fought it for several years, she ultimately lost her battle.

Shortly afterward, the family decided it was time to remove Jan's belongings from the house. Neil wasn't sure he was ready yet, but he reluctantly agreed. He sat on the bed and watched his daughters rummage through the closet, removing all of Jan's clothes. Watch. That's all he could bring himself to do—and even that was extremely difficult. At one point, his oldest daughter came across the old knitted blue cap. She turned around, holding it toward him, and said, "I remember this. You wore it all the time when I was little."

Neil seized the cap. His eyes reddened, and tears streamed relentlessly down his cheeks. His daughter sat down beside him, put her arm around his back, and rested her head on his shoulder.

"It's okay, Dad," she said. "They're only clothes. We're still keeping Mom in our hearts."

Neil looked down at the floor to hide his grief, but he nodded his acknowledgment.

"Hello . . ." A voice called from the other room. It was Neil's mom, stopping by to cook dinner. Her mother had come along as well. They all sat down in the living room. Neil looked over at his grandmother and contemplated how lucky he was that she was still around. Not only was she in her nineties, but she was still very witty. He sulkily contemplated how ironic it was that his wife hadn't outlived his grandmother. Jan should still be there, he thought; her life was short-changed and, therefore, so was his.

His grandma interrupted his brooding. "Neil, do you care if I have that knitting bag over there? It's not yours, is it?"

"No, you can have it."

Of course it wasn't his. The question was just a way to avoid mentioning that it had been Jan's and that she wouldn't need it anymore. Actually, he was surprised that his grandma wanted it. He didn't think her fingers were as operational as her intellect. However, he knew she had knitted frequently in her youth. Maybe she'd get some use from it.

As he reached down to get the bag for her, he noticed several skeins of blue and cream yarn inside with about six inches of knitted rows resting on top. Jan had renewed her knitting hobby after becoming confined indoors. He recalled walking in on her unexpectedly one day and seeing her working with the blue yarn. She quickly put it away as if she was embarrassed. Unfortunately, she didn't finish what-ever she had started, and now it would never be completed.

Neil handed the bag to his grandma, who looked happy and eager to take it. Apparently it meant more to her than he thought.

Neil wished he could be happy, yet even if he could, he wouldn't. It didn't seem right. How could he feel happi-ness when Jan was robbed of the same privilege?

Eventually it was time to face his first Christmas without Jan. Being together with the rest of the family was enjoyable, but it also made it extremely obvious that Jan was missing. He looked around at the decorations. His children had bought him a tree after realizing that he wasn't going to. Then they got out the Christmas boxes and put up the familiar adornments. Although he didn't feel like celebrating, he appreciated their attempt to raise his spirits.

Everything was in its usual place just like every other year, but Jan's absence made the celebration awkward. They were doing things differently. Anything Jan had usually done had to be absorbed by someone else. It also took longer to get anything started, similar to the way activities are delayed when waiting for a late guest to arrive. Then the realization would sink in that everyone was already there.

After dinner it was time for presents. Neil wasn't in the mood for gifts, but he could tell that everyone had put more thought into them this year—especially his. Instead of socks and cologne, he received pictures, concert tickets, an original poem, and a book about baseball, his favorite pastime.

Finally, the only gift left to open was the one from his grandma. It was soft and rectangular—probably a sweater. She usually didn't spend much, but she probably wanted to give him something special this year. He began tearing off the paper. His spirits started to rise as he realized what was inside: a magnificent blue-and-cream afghan.

Neil held it up and asked his grandma in disbelief, "Did you make this?"

She nodded her head, smiling proudly.

"I didn't think you could."

"It wasn't easy. My eyesight's bad, and my hands ache, but that little knitting bag caught my eye for a reason. It contained the beginning of an afghan I knew Jan was making for you. It's as much from her as it is from me, you know."

He did know. Jan began their life together with a knitted gift of love, and near the end of her life she had tried to make another such loving gift for him. Even though she wasn't able to finish it herself, his grandma had somehow gotten the message to get the afghan ready for him by Christmas.

Neil brought the afghan to his face, caressing it. Jan's presence overcame him in a sweep of joy, and he could feel her smiling down on him. She had helped him get through this Christmas, and Neil knew then that her love would be with him forever.

Christmas Wonder

I will astound these people with wonder upon wonder (Isaiah 29:14 NIV).

God's miracles astound us when we see them. They are full of wonder and mystery. We don't understand them, nor can we explain them. We are fascinated by them, surprised by them, frightened, or delighted by them. And the miracle of Christ, the Son of God, born to a virgin on earth is so full of wonder that we bow in reverence and awe when we remember Him. It's no surprise, then, that the Bible says, "His name is Wonderful!"

The New Doll

BETTY R. GRAHAM

*C*hristmas has always been special for me, especially when I was a little girl. For weeks before the holiday I was agog with anticipation. It didn't matter that we had very little money in our family. Since my parents insisted that we would each come up with a gift for each of our siblings, even if we had to make them, as the youngest of six children, I was assured of plenty of presents, and I worked hard to make all my offerings for the family.

I was what they called a tomboy. I'd much rather play cowboys and Indians with the neighborhood boys than play with dolls. Nevertheless, I insisted on asking for a doll each Christmas, even though I'd only play with it for about a week, and then it would sit untouched for the rest of the year.

One December, a week before Christmas, we learned that our church was gathering items to be given to the poor families of our town. Mom was making a batch of her famous beef patties as her donation. When she asked what I would give, it surprised me. *I'm just a little girl,* I thought. *What could I give?*

Then she suggested that I might donate last year's doll, which was almost as new as when I'd received it. I was shocked. I didn't want to give up my only doll, and for the first time I wondered what had happened to all the old dolls I'd received in previous years. (I didn't know then that my mother would reoutfit the last year's doll with new clothes she'd made to match the doll I'd picked out in Montgomery Ward's toy department.) And since I only had eyes for the "new" doll for such a short time, I never even missed the "old" ones.

"But, Mom, I don't want to give away my doll," I said, pouting.

"You never play with it," she said, "and some little girl might never have a doll of her own. You think about it."

"Okay," I promised, and I did think a lot about it, but my heart wasn't really in it. *After all,* I thought, *it's mine.* Maybe I should have played with it more. I thought for most of the rest of the day. I still didn't want to give up my doll, but I didn't want Mom or Santa to be mad at me. *Maybe I can ask Santa for a new doll again this year,* I thought.

Finally I agreed to do it. I held my doll all afternoon, the first time since January that I'd played with her. Her dress was clean and crisp, as it was the day I received it. By suppertime I carried her downstairs and reluctantly gave her to Mom.

"I'm proud of you," Mom said. "You will make some little girl very happy." Her words helped a little, but I couldn't honestly feel good about my loss.

On Christmas Eve, there was a knock at the door, but no one was there when Mom answered it. Sitting on the porch was a big box filled with presents and food. There were some cookies and even some of Mom's beef patties, as well as gifts for everyone in the family. It was the first time I realized that we were considered poor.

But the most amazing thing to me was my gift. When I tore off the paper, I couldn't believe my eyes, for there in all her glory was my doll, the one I'd given up. It seemed like a miracle to me.

In the years since then, I've often thought how fortunate I have been, and I try to give to those less fortunate than I with a happy heart. Give and it shall be given unto you, if not in material ways, as it was for me, in the joy received when you make someone else happy.

The Monticello Miracle

JUSTIN RODRIQUEZ

*B*ells tolled last week for December 7, 1941—the date that lives in infamy. This story starts the day after.

Young patriots rushed to the nation's defense. Don Karkos tagged along after school as his older brother, Eddie, went to enlist at the Navy recruiting station in Lewiston, Maine. The boy hunched in the back of the room as Eddie answered questions and filled out paperwork. A recruiter barked out at Don, "Hey, kid, whatsa matter, you don't like the Navy?"

"Sir, I'm not old enough," Don told him. "I don't turn seventeen until Friday."

"Good enough," snapped the recruiter.

Seaman Don Karkos shipped out of Boston and sailed into the North Atlantic. He was on the *USS Rapaden*, a tanker whose mission was to skirt the German U-boats off the English coast and refuel Allied battleships. On a warm morning in the summer of 1942, Karkos was on the *Rapaden* deck when there was a loud explosion. Twisted metal flew everywhere. Something heavy hit the boy above his right eye, cutting his forehead open.

When Karkos woke up, he was in a military hospital in Iceland. Doctors told him he would never see out of his right eye again. They wanted to remove the right eye. Karkos said, "No. Might as well leave it in, just for looks."

Karkos returned home to Lisbon Falls, Maine, a small mill town with a woolery. He worked in the mill's weave room for three years, not leaving until he paid off the mortgage on his father's house.

Karkos never regained sight in his right eye. It severely limited his peripheral vision. He'd bump into walls, never knowing what was coming around the corner. He had to be extra careful, because if anything happened to his good eye, he'd be completely blind.

But Don Karkos lived in a time when you farmed the acre you were handed and plowed forward. He married and raised a family. He started his own roofing and sheet-metal business. Karkos loved the pastoral majesty of horses and in 1978 bought his own twenty-two-acre horse farm in Harris.

Just three years ago, doctors told him that even with all the modern medical advances, he would never see in his right eye. That scared this aging man. He already had cataracts removed from his left eye.

Karkos turned eighty-two yesterday. He's been at Monticello Raceway for sixteen years. He's a paddock security guard, checking in the horses before races. He helps out in the barn.

Recently, he was preparing a horse named My Buddy Chimo for an early morning workout in paddock H. Karkos was adjusting the buxton around the horse's chest when My Buddy Chimo lowered his head quickly, came up and butted Karkos. Hit him flush in the head, straight above his right eye, his blind eye.

The old man was thrown against the wall and tried to gather himself. *I've been in a lot of fights,* he thought, *but I've never been hit that hard.* Last time he was hit with such might was on that Navy ship sixty-four years ago.

Karkos got home that night, still a little woozy. He walked down the hallway of his Monticello home, rubbing his good eye. Wait. What was happening?

Some people call it a freak coincidence; some call it fate; others call it God. And life becomes so much wider, you look at it differently.

Ask Don Karkos, who stood there in his hallway with his hand over his good eye. He could still see.

What the explosions of war had taken away, My Buddy Chimo had given back. Karkos can now see with both eyes.

He can see the wide horizon, the halo of the sunset, what's coming around the corner, which on this morning happens to be My Buddy Chimo.

"I love that horse," said Don Karkos. "Hey, right now, I'm loving it all."

Ordinary People

NANCY B. GIBBS

As the Christmas season of 1996 was quickly approaching, I wasn't listening to Christmas carols, decorating the house, or baking Christmas cookies. As a matter of fact, I dreaded Christmas. Two months earlier my father's doctor informed us that Daddy probably wouldn't live another twelve months. If the doctor was right, this would be Daddy's last Christmas. While I wanted to make the best of the holiday, the dread of the coming event filled my soul.

Because Daddy needed around-the-clock medical care, he resided in a long-term-care facility.

"Everybody needs to be able to go home for Christmas," I told my husband, Roy. We evaluated how much money it would take for Daddy to spend the day at home. We would have to rent a hospital bed. Daddy would have to be transported by ambulance, since he couldn't ride in a car. We would have to hire a nurse to come to stay with him.

After the figures were totaled, I realized I didn't have nearly enough money to take Daddy home for Christmas. One morning, as I drove the sixty-plus miles to visit with Daddy in his nursing home room, I heard an important announcement on the radio. The deejay mentioned that the station would be making twelve wishes come true that Christmas.

"My dream is simply too big," I said aloud in my car. Then the Bible verse in Luke 1:37 (NIV) came to my mind. "For nothing is impossible with God."

As I drove the remainder of the way to the nursing home, I prayed. "Please God," I begged, "help us to take Daddy home for Christmas."

That night after I returned home from my trip, I wrote a letter to the radio station. I explained my father's terminal illness, how we had always spent Christmas Eve together in his home, and how my greatest wish was to take Daddy home one more time. I listed what it would take to make my wish come true. I never expected the impossible, but in my heart, I remembered that all things are possible with God. The next day, I said a prayer and dropped my letter in the mailbox.

Several days passed. I received a telephone call at work. "Your wish is coming true," the deejay announced. For a few seconds I was speechless. All the plans to take Daddy home for Christmas were already made. A medical supply company would donate a hospital bed. A medical transportation company had agreed to take Daddy home that morning and then back to the nursing home that night. A nurse, who was also a young mother, agreed to spend Christmas Eve with us that year.

A few things happened healthwise with Daddy that caused us to worry that he wouldn't be able to make the trip. Daddy spent several days the week before Christmas in the hospital. But two days before Christmas Eve, God performed a miracle. He made Daddy well enough to go home.

On Christmas Eve morning, I met the ambulance at the nursing home. I rode along humming Christmas carols. My heart felt like it would explode with joy. My greatest wish was coming true. My mom had gotten busy and decorated the house. When we arrived, I walked beside the stretcher as the technicians carried Daddy inside. When Daddy saw his home, tears filled his eyes. There wasn't a dry eye in the house, including the eyes of the nurse and the medical technicians.

That Christmas Eve was a day that I will never forget.

Not only did my father go home one last time, I saw an awesome amount of love as it poured from the hearts of many people. The deejays, a young nurse, two medical technicians, and the owners of a medical supply company gave freely of their hearts to make my greatest Christmas wish come true. I was then and forever will be grateful for their generosity.

I experienced that day what I already knew. Nothing is impossible with God. I also discovered that God uses ordinary people like you and me to make heartfelt Christmas wishes come true.

A Christmas to Remember

DON DWIGHT

A year ago Christmas Day, my relatives and friends back in the States were singing "Silent Night" and "Joy to the World." But those weren't the words on my lips. A beautiful calm morning on a resort island in Thailand had been interrupted by screams of grief. The tidal wave of sadness would soon wash against the rest of the globe.

We arrived on Phi Phi Island off the coast of Thailand's mainland on the morning of December 25. It was a dream vacation we'd looked forward to for months. To celebrate our twenty-fifth wedding anniversary, I'd saved up to be able to take my wife, Lillian, away for a memorable getaway. Since we are missionaries with the Evangelical Covenant Church in Taiwan, I'd been saving for a while.

When Lillian pointed out we had frequent-flier miles

to use up, she suggested we take our five children with us. I thought it was a great idea. Since our oldest son attends college in California, it seemed like a perfect way to experience a family Christmas to remember. Besides, I really couldn't imagine celebrating this special milestone in our marriage without our kids.

We left Taipei on December 21 and flew to Bangkok. After a couple of days touring the city, we traveled by train for thirteen hours down country. Although my kids have traveled more than most, they were wide-eyed by what they saw. On Christmas Eve we tried our best to recreate our holiday traditions in our hotel room. I read the account of Jesus' birth from the Bible and then we exchanged small gifts we'd purchased for each other in the marketplace earlier in the day.

On Christmas morning Lillian and I surprised our children by taking them to a place where they could ride elephants. Even though it meant coughing up quite a few bucks, we wanted to give them a Christmas they'd never forget. Later that afternoon we took an hour and a half ferry ride to the tropical island where we'd spend the balance of our vacation.

The idyllic setting of Phi Phi Island was one of the

main reasons Lillian and I had selected it as our destination. The beaches were like white powder. The water was the most breathtaking blue I'd ever seen. The picturesque cottages on the beach were just as the travel brochures had portrayed.

As my family and I made our way from the ferry landing to our hotel, we were shown three bungalows on the side of the hill overlooking the water about a hundred yards from the beach. My kids looked up to me with a knowing glance. They knew that three months earlier when I first made the reservations, I'd attempted to book bungalows next to the picturesque surf. I had to break the news to the kids back then that all those rooms were already taken for Christmas week. I was just as disappointed as they were.

After settling into our rooms, we put on our bathing suits and walked down to the beach for a swim. The water was so transparent and tranquil the kids didn't want to get out. But since it was starting to get dark, and we hadn't had dinner yet, I promised the family we could go back first thing in the morning. As it turned out that was a promise I wasn't able to keep.

The next morning, we wandered down the path to

have breakfast at the hotel restaurant on the beach. The sky was clear and blue just like the calm water. We made plans about how we'd spend the day. Snorkeling was at the top of everyone's list. As we walked back up the hill, we paused to drink in the beauty of the setting.

About a half hour later, I heard the sound of people yelling. I stood at the door to our bungalow and noticed some smoke at the top of our hill. Assuming it was a brushfire and nothing more, I encouraged our kids to get their swimsuits on. But as we started down toward the beach, it was obvious something wasn't right. Getting closer we saw that the hotel restaurant where we'd eaten an hour before was destroyed.

All the evidence pointed to a massive tsunami. There was debris and large pieces of furniture on the beach and floating in the water. At that point I was completely unaware that other portions of the island had been hit even harder than where we were. I had no way of knowing that upwards of eleven hundred people had been killed in a few minutes' time.

I told the kids there was no way we could go swimming because something terrible had happened. We stood with a sense of disbelief realizing that all the beachside bungalows had been swept away. The very bungalows we had attempted to stay in were gone.

In a few minutes several people carried the limp body of a woman up from the surf and laid her down in front of where our family was standing. It was obvious she wasn't breathing. A man who appeared to be the woman's husband and her young son stood in shock beside her.

When no one responded to my screams to start CPR, Lillian and I began frantically to try and revive the woman. Soon other onlookers spelled us, including our college-age son. Sadly, after doing mouth-to-mouth resuscitation for an hour, we had to admit our efforts were not going to bring her back.

My wife and I introduced ourselves to the woman's husband and son. We discovered they were tourists from England. Lillian and I wrapped our arms around them both and asked the Lord to comfort them with a peace He alone could give. I felt the Holy Spirit nudging me to help them find ways to return home with an occupied casket.

Later in the day as we walked the island, the devastation of the tsunami's impact hit home. Shops were leveled and the doctors' clinic was destroyed. We knew we had to make immediate plans to try and evacuate the island. The following morning we made our way on foot to the ferry landing. A distance that had taken fifteen minutes two days earlier now took an hour. Dodging debris was a challenge. The corpses that had not yet been removed were unnerving.

Once we reached the dock, I was overwhelmed by the sight of several hundred other tourists attempting to leave the island. As we waited for a fleet of ferries to gradually rescue those stranded on the devastated island, I reflected on the gift of life.

I didn't know exactly why God spared our family, but my heart was filled with immense gratitude for the chance to be alive. Had we gotten the accommodations we wanted, we'd be dead. Had we gone to breakfast thirty minutes later, we likely would not have survived.

Unlike Christmas presents piled beneath a tree, life truly is priceless. In addition, it can't be taken for granted. None of those who perished on Phi Phi Island knew December 26 would be their last day. I plan to use this special gift of life which God has given me to serve Him the rest of my days.

Star of Wonder

RICHARD H. SCHNEIDER

O star of wonder, star of night, star with royal beauty bright . . ."

That refrain haunted me as I gazed up into the glittering night while walking home from church with my parents and brothers on a long-ago Christmas Eve. *What was it really, that mysterious star of God?* I wondered.

So have many others wondered. For of all the biblical records of Christ's birth, it is the star of Bethlehem that has especially piqued our interest, and the imagination of poets, painters, and composers.

Just what was this stellar body that guided "We Three Kings"? Through the years that question has continued to intrigue me. It has sent me to a variety of sources, including the Christmas star show at Chicago's Adler Planetarium, where I watched the projector turn the great dark dome into the sky over Bethlehem as it was seen two thousand years ago.

As I studied books and theories, I learned that some theologians believe the star was a supernatural event, some consider the story purely symbolic, and others have searched for a natural event in the sky such as a supernova (exploding star) or flaming comet. A number of scholars have suggested it was a conjunction, or lining up of several planets. The consensus, however, is that we probably may never know.

In recent years, several scholarly studies of the star have been made, and I've read them avidly. One, by Dr. Ernest L. Martin, a California Bible-historian, especially fascinated me. "The Birth of Christ Recalculated" is based on modern discoveries in history, archaeology, and astronomy. Of all the theories currently clustering around the Christmas star, I believe Martin's may be the most plausible.

The story of the star starts with the only people known to have beheld it: Matthew's "wise men from the east" (Matthew 2:1). In the gospel's original Greek, the word for wise men was *magoi*, or magi. These, I learned, were probably a group of Zoroastrian priests from Mesopotamia (today's Iraq) in the ancient Parthian Empire, hundreds of miles east of Jerusalem. Skilled astronomers, the *magoi* carefully studied the heavens from atop great terraced temples or ziggurats.

God warns us against using astrology, and the Jews of that day received His warning in the Old Testament. However, the Parthian wise men often interpreted celestial events as omens. As religious scholars they would have known the Jewish prophecies of a coming "messiah king." A major Hebrew religious school already existed in their area. In fact, their own religion predicted a "great deliverer," not necessarily of their own faith.

We also know that the *magoi* were excellent scientists. I was impressed by their skill when I learned that a clay tablet from 7 BC found in Mesopotamia forecast acccurately the movements of the planets for the following year. To the *magoi,* incidentally, star could mean almost any light in the sky, whether star, planet, comet, or nova.

Today's astronomers, by using current data and computers, can depict accurately the position of a star or a planet centuries ago! Thus, with the help of a planetarium projector, one can actually see what the sky looked like on any night of the year—any year!

Modern astronomers are certain that something remarkable took place in the Middle Eastern sky beginning in the summer of 3 BC. It was a most dramatic display, and the *magoi*, those expert watchers of the sky, would certainly have seen it.

What made my growing knowledge of the star all the more fascinating was learning that experts such as Dr. Martin believe that this unusual celestial event occurred right around the time of Jesus' birth, now generally considered to have been sometime in 3 or 2 BC.

Just what was this momentous display that so captured the attention of the wise men? With mounting interest I read what they would have seen.

At dawn on August 12, 3 BC, the *magoi* stood atop their ziggurats, watching raptly as the two shining planets Jupiter and Venus rose in conjunction in the eastern sky. Conjunctions (which had a tremendous significance in their eyes) occur when celestial bodies line up so closely that, although they are actually millions of miles apart, they appear to us as a single, superbright light. To the wise men, Jupiter signified kingship; Venus, birth and motherhood. In other words, the conjunction meant that somewhere a king was being born. But king of what people? The wise men had an answer: the conjunction occurred in the constellation of Leo—to the *magoi* the symbol of the Hebrew tribe of Judah.

But there was even more to come, I discovered.

Ten months later, in June of 2 BC, it happened again. Once more Jupiter and Venus lined up, this time so close they blazed as a single, glorious light. But now they shone in the evening sky, in the west. To the astounded wise men, that was precisely the direction of Jerusalem, capital city of Hebrew kings.

Nor was that all. Between these two dazzling planetary displays, some other unique heavenly events took place. In September of 3 BC the excited wise men saw Jupiter rise to meet Regulus, the bright star in the constellation Leo, and a symbol of rulership. To their wonder, this occurred twice more, in February and May of 2 BC. To the *magoi,* these three conjunctions, preceded and followed by the Jupiter/Venus conjunctions, could mean only one thing: the birth of a very powerful Jewish king.

And so they journeyed—over "field and fountain, moor and mountain"—on a month-long westward pilgrimage, anxious to find the new king and pay him homage. On the map, I eagerly followed their caravan's probable route north along the wide Euphrates River, then across to Antioch, down the Mediterranean coast and up to Jerusalem in the mountainous highlands of Judaea.

Finally they arrived at Herod's palace, asking to see the

king's new son—"He that is born King of the Jews" (Matthew 2:2). But the surprised king had no son, and in a paranoid frenzy he called together his chief priests and scribes and "demanded of them where Christ should be born" (2:4). They replied, "In Bethlehem of Judaea" (2:5).

So the wise men set out for the little town of Bethlehem, five miles south. As caravans would do, they probably started out at dawn—and were astonished to see the same blazing star that had first called them on their journey! For, as astronomical calculations show, in early September of 2 BC Jupiter and Venus again rose in conjunction, glowing brightly in the Bethlehem dawn. In my search, I read where some interpreters point to an appearance of Jupiter over Bethlehem on December 25, 2 BC. But I personally feel drawn to the Jupiter and Venus conjunction in September of 2 BC because it was so strikingly similar to the conjunction that had launched the *magoi's* quest. Furthermore, Matthew 2:10 tells us that on beholding their old friend, the wise men "rejoiced with exceeding great joy." I could sense their excitement as they urged their camel caravan, clinking and clanking, onward to Bethlehem.

The *magoi* would probably have had little trouble finding the holy family in Bethlehem, for the dramatic events of Jesus' birth—angels appearing, astonished shepherds—

would have been common local knowledge. And so the wise men from the east, lured westward by the heavens they were so skilled at observing, finally and triumphantly came to stand before Jesus Christ.

Though these current astronomical explanations of the star of the magi seem convincing, I realize that we'll never know for sure. Were the extraordinary conjunctions of 3 BC and 2 BC just coincidences? Or was a divine plan working through them?

This Christmas Eve as I look up through the cold clear night to God's glorious firmament, I know it will probably always be a mystery, this "star of wonder." Yet—although I, as a Christian, do not need material evidence to support my faith— I am sure of one thing: two thousand years ago, something wonderful in the heavens did, indeed, brighten the night sky over Bethlehem . . .

> O star of wonder, star of night,
> Star with royal beauty bright;
> Westward leading, still proceeding,
> Guide us to Thy perfect light.

Robbie

MARY CHANDLER

A stone crashed through the glass. I rushed to my kitchen window just in time to see the boy in the familiar navy jacket dart around the corner and disappear. *Not again,* I thought. *Not after all my saving and planning.*

Struggling to pay my husband Don's rising tuition at Northwestern dental school in Chicago, we had moved into subsidized housing. My initial introduction to the family downstairs had not gone well. The morning we moved in, Anne, a thin, gaunt woman with straggly brown hair, wearing a long, black dress, smiled and introduced herself and her two children, Sherilyn, eleven, and Robbie, nine. When Sherilyn saw Michael, our nine-month-old baby, tears welled up in her eyes and fell onto her ruddy cheeks. Robbie glared at Michael and punched his arm. While I cradled my sobbing baby, Anne smacked Robbie, shouted a few choice words, apologized, and herded her kids into her apartment.

167

"That's it, Don," I told my husband. "I can do without neighbors like that." I avoided Anne and her brood like the plague, but Robbie never let up.

Icy winds from Lake Michigan ripped through my winter coat as I walked from the Blue Cross office where I worked to catch the bus. By the time I picked up Michael from the nearby babysitter, I was chilled to the bone and in no mood for pranks. Opening my screen door I found a dead squirrel, frozen stiff, still in the rattrap. Robbie, his tattered navy jacket wrapped around his skinny body, stepped out from behind a tree, smirking. I ignored him.

The next Saturday the sun finally came out. I hung diapers on the clothesline behind Anne's apartment. Two hours later, while Michael slept, I automatically unhooked each clothespin, gathering the diapers into my arms as fast as I could, without looking up. When I got to the last diaper, something brushed my hair. A dead rat hung by its tail from the final clothespin. I screamed. Robbie stood at his window, making faces and laughing. I was seething. I hate rats, and I hated that kid even more. I pounded on their apartment door. No one answered.

Snow blanketed the barren ground. It was knee-deep and still falling. That's when the snowballs started. Robbie heaved them at my kitchen panes, after molding the snow around a marble. He never missed. *He should be a pitcher for the Cubs,* I thought. My pleading made no difference. He'd sneer, blow on his bare hands, form another snowball, and let it fly.

Just before Christmas, Michael caught the flu. His temperature soared to 106. Don was working two jobs and wouldn't be home all weekend. With no phone, I was desperate. I cradled my listless baby and knocked on Anne's door. "I need to call a doctor," I said.

Wrinkled clothes covered every corner of their home, with more piled on the sofa. Roaches scurried in and out of open cereal boxes, through the sugar, across the floors, and up the walls. Anne, wearing a dismal black dress, handed me the phone. By the time my conversation with the doctor ended, I was in tears.

"The kids are visiting their auntie," Anne said. "I'm coming up to help you."

I didn't argue. We undressed Michael and laid him on a blanket on the floor. Anne helped me cover his hot skin with lukewarm kitchen towels, again and again, until his fever finally broke and he fell asleep.

"I wanted to be a nurse," Anne said. "But my husband ran off after my last baby died." Tears filled her eyes. "The baby lived eight months."

"I'm so sorry, Anne."

"That's why I wear black. For Patrick." She paused. "Sherilyn can't look at babies without crying," Anne said, wiping her eyes, "and Robbie's mad at the whole world." She pushed her hair back from her face. "Anytime you need me," Anne said, "knock on the floor. I'll come right up."

The next day Anne cornered the Italian fruit peddler, bought "slightly bruised" peaches, and brought us some peach cobbler. Three weeks later Sherilyn delivered chocolate chip cookies. When Michael saw those cookies, he giggled and reached out to Sherilyn, his dark brown eyes shining.

"My baby brother's in heaven," she said, looking at her scuffed black shoes.

"I know. Your mom told me. I'm so sorry." I put my arm around her shoulder. "I think Michael wants to play with you. Would you like to stay for a while?"

She nodded.

While Sherilyn warmed up to me, Robbie never did; in fact, he went out of his way to avoid me. His pranks didn't stop. Finally, I began to formulate a plan.

Tuition came due again; we struggled to pay our bills. Yet, each month I set a few dollars aside, squeezing our budget to the max. Meanwhile, I found sugar on my stoop, Vaseline smeared on my doorknobs, and raw eggs dripping on my outside walls. My patience was nearly exhausted. When that stone crashed through the window, breaking the glass, I felt like breaking Robbie's neck. Instead, I gritted my teeth and rushed downstairs.

"Anne," I said, "I need your help."

Her eyes avoided mine. "I'll pay for the window," she said.

"It's not that. Tell Robbie the mailman left something for him over at my place and that he'll have to come and get it."

"All right—but I don't know if he'll come." She stared at the sycamore where Robbie was hiding. "He's afraid you'll call the police."

I laughed. "I don't have a phone, remember?"

Robbie came over. His tousled hair looked as though he'd caught it in a lawnmower. He had long outgrown his holey jeans, and his wrinkled red T-shirt dwarfed his thin frame.

"Whatcha want?" he asked, looking everywhere but at me.

"I've seen you playing baseball with the other boys," I said. "How would you like to go to a Chicago Cubs game?"

"For real?"

I nodded. "I'm taking you, Sherilyn, and your mom. The game's next Saturday."

He cocked his head. "You're coming?"

"Yup. I've never seen the Cubs play," I winked. "Besides, I've been saving up for popcorn, sodas, hot dogs—the works—and a special surprise for you and Sherilyn." I paused. "You do like the Cubs, don't you?"

"Man, oh man! I love 'em! I've never been to a game either."

"I've got bus tokens," Anne said that Saturday as we headed for the bus stop. At Wrigley Field we found our seats—up high, but in the center section. The kids sat between Anne and me. The Cubs came to bat.

"Batter up!" Robbie shouted. He jumped up and assumed a batting stance. "Kapow!" he yelled as the ball flew into center field. "Will ya look at that! A double on the first pitch!"

"Popcorn! Peanuts! Candy!" the vendor hollered. I gave Anne a twenty. "Buy the kids whatever they want," I said. "I'll be right back."

"Here," I told Robbie and Sherilyn when I returned, handing each of them a Cubs T-shirt and a cap.

Robbie peeled off his shirt, replaced it with the new

one, and plopped his cap on his head. Sherilyn pulled her T-shirt over her tank top and slid her long blond ponytail through the back slit of her Cubs cap.

Don't ask me who played against the Cubs that afternoon or to name any of the players on the team. I didn't really see that game. All I saw were two kids in T-shirts and Chicago Cubs caps, stuffing their faces, jumping up and down, and shouting their lungs out.

Amazingly, after that day, the stone-throwing stopped. So did the other pranks. A few days later, Anne showed up at my door wearing a bright blue dress, her hair clean and curled. Sherilyn and Robbie played with Michael. We had picnics on the lawn, and Don and I invited the kids to go with us to the Shedd Aquarium and the Field Museum of Natural History. That whole summer I never saw Robbie without his baseball cap. I would have sworn it was glued to his head.

For Christmas we got him a ball and bat.

Now, years later, what I remember most about Chicago is the family downstairs—especially a hurting boy who acted in the shadows until the light of kindness helped him to shine.

Stranger at Table #5

CORYNE WONG-COLLINSWORTH

*I*t was five days before Christmas, and the café where I worked in northern California glowed with strands of red and green chili peppers. Holiday music played over the sound system, and my coworkers excitedly discussed their plans. "Doing anything special?" they asked me. I shook my head no.

I was three thousand miles from my family in Hawaii, pursuing my lifelong dream of becoming a pediatric nurse. I attended classes all day, then went straight to my full-time waitress job at night. My weekly schedule had left me exhausted and extremely homesick.

I had always looked forward to the holidays. But this December I felt unable to go on. In my prayers I told God that if I could just get home to see my mom, dad, and brothers, I could survive the next two years until I graduated. But how? Rent, tuition, textbooks, and other expenses left me with no extra cash. Money to go home? I barely had money to eat.

"I'm on my break. Cover for me, will you?" asked Maribelle, another waitress, as she passed me on her way to the employees' lounge. "By the way, there's this guy at table five," she said. "He's been sitting there for more than an hour, not making any trouble but not ordering anything either." She paused. "It's like he's . . . waiting for somebody."

I looked in the corner. Sure enough, there was a slim, pleasant-looking man dressed in worn Levi's, a red-and-black plaid shirt, and a black baseball cap, just sitting, alone. I went over, trying to muster a smile. "I'm Cory," I said. "Please let me know if you want anything."

I was turning to walk away when the man spoke. He had a soft, low voice, but somehow I could hear it clearly and plainly in the noisy restaurant. "I'd like an order of nachos," he said, "and a glass of water."

My heart sank. The nachos were the cheapest thing on the menu, which meant I wouldn't get much of a tip. But maybe this guy was broke, and I sure knew how that felt. So I tried my best to make him feel okay. "Coming right up," I said. I returned a few minutes later and slid the nachos in front of him. "That will be two dollars and ninety-five cents."

He reached into his pocket and handed me a single bill. "Keep the change," he said quietly.

I looked—then looked again. "Excuse me, sir," I said. "This is a hundred-dollar bill."

"I know," he replied gently.

My eyes opened wide. "I don't understand," I said. "What do you want from me?"

"Not a thing," he said, looking straight into my eyes. He stood up. "Call your mother tonight," he said. "Merry Christmas." Then he moved off in the direction of the front door. When I turned to thank him, he was nowhere in sight, although the exit was at least fifty feet away.

The rest of the evening passed in a blur. I finished work, went back to my apartment and put the money on the table. I had just turned on the television when the phone rang. It was my mother! She announced that my brothers had bought an airline ticket to get me home for Christmas. But they could only afford the fare one way. "Can you possibly manage the other part of the ticket?" she asked.

At that moment a commercial flashed on television. A major airline was announcing cut-rate fares to Hawaii, one way for ninety-nine dollars! I jumped off the sofa, shouting, "Thank you, God. I'm going home!"

That was seven years ago. Because of that visit to my family, I returned to my studies filled with a new spirit and determination. Today I'm a registered nurse, caring for sick children. And every Christmas my husband, John, and I try to do something for someone else, just as the man at table number five had done for me. One year we purchased packages of warm socks and, with the wind howling at our backs, crept along the creek and handed them out to the people without homes who resided on the banks. The following Christmas we organized a blanket drive; and as the homeless gathered around a campfire wrapped in their new blankets, John asked each one to reflect on the tiny babe whose birthday it was.

Whether creeping along creek beds, tiptoeing down hospital corridors to hang stockings, or secretly leaving gifts of food (who knows where this Christmas will find us?), I always think of the mysterious stranger at table five who helped me.

In my time of need he appeared—no halo or sparkling wings, but a sort of angel just the same. And that is the kind of angel we all can be.

$\mathcal{P}$eace and Goodwill

Glory to God in the highest, and on earth peace, goodwill toward men! (Luke 2:14 NKJV).

*P*eace. God's plan was to bring peace to the world through His Son, Jesus. And yet, His coming created great strife among the people. Did His plan fail? Not at all. For those of us who believe in Jesus, the Prince of Peace, we find that blessed spiritual peace and enjoy its soothing comfort in our lives. For those who don't believe in Him, strife and struggle mark their way. Perhaps, by our showing them His peace through our good will toward them, they will be attracted to Him and find His comforting peace too. That's our task. That's our joy. We are peacemakers.

Christmas Eve Miracle

DARLENE FRANKLIN

I studied our living room window with satisfaction. Scotch tape held up a single strand of miniature lights that glittered off a multi-colored garland. Artificial snow made up for the brown ground to be expected from a Texas winter where the idea of a "white Christmas" amounted to an oxymoron.

I loved the trappings of Christmas, whatever their origin. I especially loved the Christmas tree, its evergreen branches reminding me of the eternal life that is mine because of the gift God gave on the first Christmas. But this year we would not have a tree. We couldn't afford it. So instead I decorated the window.

I set up an old folding table in front of the window and spread a holiday tablecloth over the top. Together with my toddler, Jaran, I tucked cookie cutters under blank newsprint and rubbed red and green crayons over the raised surfaces. Soon a profusion of stars, Santa Clauses and candy canes appeared on enough paper for the few presents we would exchange.

I tucked Jaran into bed for his afternoon nap. While he slept, I used our newly-crafted wrapping paper to prepare the presents I had found for my family at a dollar store. I included a nutcracker with a bag of nuts in the shell, together with a note, "I hope this present is all it's cracked up to be." A mention of "the time of our lives" went with a green timer. A box of new crayons, construction paper, and a set of miniature plastic tools represented our gifts for Jaran.

God had already seen to our biggest Christmas present. The student housing we rented had a stove with two working burners but no oven. I missed being able to bake and we had all grown tired of pan-fried food.

My husband made numerous entries to a contest sponsored by the *Ft. Worth Star Telegram*. We dreamed of winning the Hawaiian vacation, the way we'd hope for Ed McMann to show up at our doorstep. For the cost of a stamp, we bought a dream. We didn't get the Hawaiian vacation, but God provided the prize that we needed: a microwave oven. Turkey remained out of the question, but visions of chicken and roasts danced in my head. We could have an honest-to-goodness Christmas meal! What more could we ask for? We had already examined our limited finances and decided against the expense of a tree, opting for a simple meal and a limited number of gifts.

God must have seen my heart, lonely for my own family, thousands of miles away in Maine, and even my in-laws in Oklahoma, too far to travel for a day trip with my husband's schedule.

The phone rang while I was rereading my well-worn copy of *A Christmas Carol.* It was an older couple from the large church we attended, people we had never met. "Can we come over?"

"Of course!"

A few minutes later the strangers arrived at my door, bearing a box festooned with gay wrapping paper and filled with surprises. They had a beige sweater for me, a yellow truck for Jaran, and a dress shirt for my husband, John. The food they brought made my mouth water: canned ham; candied sweet potatoes; green beans; cornbread stuffing mix; pumpkin pie. The additional canned food would keep us going for a month. Someone must have shared the paucity of our celebration and this couple— a deacon at the church—reached out to us. *This is a miracle,* I thought. *The miracle of God's love at Christmas reborn through His children.*

The couple said good-bye and continued on their way to help another family in need. I put the groceries away in the pantry and sat down at the piano we had purchased as an act of faith shortly before Jaran's birth. I adored Christmas carols and paged through my book with over a hundred familiar tunes, unable to stop with just one. Who could decide on a favorite? Not me! Did I prefer the solemn faith of "Hark! The Herald Angels Sing"? The rollicking symbolism of "I Saw Three Ships"? The Victorian feel of "God Rest Ye Merry Gentlemen"? I loved them all! Jaran woke up from his nap and joined me in making music to God. "Christmas is Jesus' birthday," we sang together.

The phone rang again. This time a family from the church where I worked part-time came by with more food. I rejoiced again in God's provision. I had to stack cans on top of cans to make room. In fact, we had so much that I felt compelled to give back. Jaran helped me pick out a tithe, one can out of every ten we had received, to pass on to people in greater need than we.

The doorbell rang. This time it was the postal carrier with a package from my parents. "Merry Christmas!" he called as he walked on to the next house. I set the package under the table, unopened. Thank God for my parents, who would make our Christmas even better.

Next on my agenda was a special family tradition: making a birthday cake for Jesus. When I heard of the idea, I decided it was a great way to help my son understand the real meaning of Christmas. Jaran and I mixed a microwave cake mix and baked a small, square cake. We frosted it and placed plastic manger figures on the top. Tomorrow morning, after we read the Christmas story from Luke, we would light the candle and sing happy birthday to Jesus.

I had done everything I could to prepare for Christmas. Christmas cards hung from a string nailed to the wall. Ornaments Jaran had made lay among the presents on the table. The birthday cake was ready, presents wrapped, and meal ready to fix tomorrow in our brand new microwave. All we needed was for John's workday to end and for him to return home.

I was fixing boxed macaroni and cheese when the front door opened. John was home. "Come out and help me!" His blue eyes danced and he couldn't stop grinning.

Hanging out of the back of our battered Dodge Dart was a live Christmas tree.

"My boss said the office didn't need it anymore, since it's Christmas Eve. He asked me if I wanted it."

I studied the slightly dry fir still tacked to a wooden

board, but I wouldn't have cared if it was as spindly as Charlie Brown's tree. It was a Christmas tree, and it was ours.

The evening sped by as we moved the lights and gar-lands from the window to the tree. Jaran's handcrafted paper doily angel went on top. I dug out paper clips and unfolded them for emergency ornament hangers. We sang to taped Christmas music as we worked: "O Christmas Tree," "Silent Night," "Away in a Manger." Next came wooden ornaments sent by my parents in con-sideration of the needs of small children. Jaran exclaimed over each one, from Santa on skis to a cradle and a train engine. We took care in hanging the precious handmade ornaments that included pictures of Jaran. Last of all, we added our two fancy ornaments, one for our first Christmas together, and one for Jaran's first Christmas.

The tree was still pretty bare. We removed Christmas cards from the string, cut off the fronts, poked holes in them and hung them on the bare branches. While we dec-orated, I told John the story of our day. I showed him the replenished pantry, told him of my plans to share the abundance, and teased him with the wrapped presents.

At last we were finished. The tree transformed the room. God had given us a Christmas miracle of everlast-ing life and love.

When Time Stood Still

ADELA ROGERS ST. JOHNS

When it comes to God's guidance, which it does every day, every hour, there are many ways we can seek it. More and more often, more and more surely, with more and more conviction as my need and my faith grow, I have learned to depend on it.

"Stand ye still."

Always those words come to me when I ask for guidance, wherever I happen to be, no matter how rushing and noisy it may be inside my mind and out. For to those words I owe the life of my oldest son, Mac.

One December night I awoke suddenly and completely, sitting straight up in bed. I was sure somebody had called me. When I switched on the light, my clock said 3:15. Getting up, I prowled—a niece, a nephew, one younger son were sleeping in the house. Everyone seemed safe and peaceful.

187

I do not hear voices nor see lights nor catch the echo of bells. But when guidance comes, something irresistible seems to take over. Now the call was distinct in my mind—a call for help.

In the living room, I saw the Christmas tree. Next to the fireplace it stood, slim and green. Tomorrow we'd hang it with bright colors and put the Christmas angel on the top—the one that had been my grandmother's. It was the season of peace on earth, goodwill to men, but there was no peace on earth this December of 1944. It was the month of the Battle of the Bulge, Bastogne, the Ardennes. My brothers were marines in the Pacific, my oldest son in France with Patton.

I went back to bed. The call was not from within my home's safe walls. The clock now said 3:25. But it was a different time on islands in the Pacific, on the battlefields of Europe. So I did what, whenever it is possible, is my first step in asking for guidance. I got my Bible from under the detective story with which I'd read myself to sleep, shut my eyes and said, "Father, let me find Your word that's meant for me. I think one of Your other children needs Your help. I am far away from whoever it is, but You are near us both. Speak to us now through Your Word."

In guidance, my experimentation leads me to believe

that inner quietness is the first requirement. And the most difficult. Nobody wants to be quiet. Not many of us want to be silent and listen. Prayer is an audience, not an audition; nevertheless, we start telling our Father about the problem and how He ought to solve it.

That's why, when I ask for guidance, to keep my own mind still, I read something: a prayer, a book of inspiration, mostly the Bible. Then I try to be quiet for as long as I am able, in my mind I mean, which is about one minute and forty-two seconds; two minutes at the most, as it is with most people. Then I ask, with all the expectation and humility that I can generate.

That night I opened the Bible. Just anywhere, where it fell open.

"Stand ye still, and see the salvation of the LORD with you . . . fear not, nor be dismayed for the LORD will be with you" (2 Chronicles 20:17 KJV).

"Stand ye still." It stood out from the page like copy on a billboard.

And so, simply and directly, I began to pray. I knew now from whom the call had come, as it had come for many years in many dark nights.

"Father," I prayed, "Your guidance now goes to my son, somewhere in battle, somewhere in danger. Your

Word goes forth to him and will accomplish what You please for him, which is his safety and his guidance, the light to his feet."

"Stand ye still."

I knew, I really did, that this was my guidance and would be my son's. That it had come to me through a channel kept open by prayer and longing and seeking. I went back to sleep in peace.

At breakfast, I told everyone what had taken place. Then it came to me that as it was so near Christmas and everybody always remembers things around Christmas, perhaps Mac would remember something about that early morning hour. So to his APO number I wrote, describing the experience.

His reply reached me soon after Christmas. It said, "Yes, I can remember. I was the leader on an I&R [Intelligence and Reconnaisance] platoon; we were out ahead of our regiment, somewhere in the German area, to see if it was safe to move forward. We were moving cautiously, but General Patton was always in a hurry; so we were trotting along as fast as we dared.

"All of a sudden it was as though something told me to stop. To stand still. And as I did, out of the corner of my eye, I saw a place on a tree where somebody had chopped off the bark and scrawled in paint the word *minen*. So I knew it was a mine field. A German soldier had put that sign up to warn his own troops.

"We went back faster than we'd come out, and called up the mine detector squad and, sure enough, there were mines enough to blow up the whole platoon, maybe the Third Army. If I hadn't stopped (and I had to be standing dead-still to see it because it faced the other way), I wouldn't be writing this letter. And we wouldn't have had any Christmas, merry or otherwise."

Maybe you will have another explanation for this!

But to this day it has made a working Christian out of my son Mac. To me it was God's guidance. The voice of His love for us coming through to us.

The first time you receive guidance you will know the difference. You can mistake rhinestones for diamonds, but you can never mistake a diamond for a rhinestone. I know what is true guidance when my mind, my consciousness, whatever we call our mental process, is thinking utterly and completely with some thought which I know I have not thought. This comes when the mind, which was in Christ Jesus for which we have prayed, takes over.

Best Christmas Gift

JOANNE K. HILL

Some miracles don't come with whistles and bells. Nor do they always happen instantly. Sometimes they evolve over time. That's how it was for my best Christmas gift.

My parents may have loved each other, but apparently, they had a hard time expressing it. They came from very different backgrounds. My mother had played in a band, and her family's home was a center of social activity. My father was more of a loner, focused on business and his religion. We had few times when just our little family did something together, and most of those times ended in a stressful silence. Finally, they separated for good.

Coming from a Christian background, I could neither understand nor accept this breakup. Even though I prayed constantly for a miracle to make our family whole once again, we were eventually driven even further apart.

Shortly after I started first grade, my brother and sister went into a foster home in an adjoining state, and I went to live with my grandmother. My father moved across the country to California. When I became an adult, I learned that shortly after my sister was born, Mom had a nervous breakdown and could not care for us.

After a couple of years living with first one relative's family, then another, I joined my siblings in the foster home. With three-fifths of us together again, I prayed harder for my parents to restore our family unit.

Then Mom met someone else, a widower with no children, and he proposed marriage. The man Mom brought to visit us seemed nice, but I wanted my real father. When Mom and Ralph brought the news of their engagement, I reacted horridly. But that didn't stop the marriage, and shortly after their wedding, they came to get the three of us children.

The week before Christmas 1943 we arrived with our belongings at a cute little bungalow in Mishawaka, Indiana. The house was lavishly decorated, and there was a huge tree in the living room. A mixture of sweet, spicy smells wafted through the rooms. Although I tried hard not to be enthusiastic, I soon caught the holiday spirit.

Ralph had little experience with young children, but I think he had a sixth sense for feelings, perhaps due to his job as a state trooper. He treated us with the same kindness and respect as he did our mother and never brought up my thoughtless behavior when I first heard of the engagement. Each day my resolve to dislike this man my mother married grew less intense.

Since we had no gifts to offer, we three children decided to put on a little play for Mom and Ralph on Christmas Eve. With Mom's help, we planned and rehearsed all day while our stepfather was at work.

After supper, Mom told Ralph to sit in his favorite chair and wait for a special surprise. In the kitchen she helped us light candles in candlesticks, then turned off all the lights, except those on the tree, and joined her new husband.

Singing "Silent Night," the three of us marched into the living room. When we finished, my little sister, Vicki, ran to Ralph, crawled up on his lap and gave him a big hug and kiss. My brother, Dick, also hugged him. I hung back.

"Who wants to help me with the hot chocolate and cookies?" Mom asked in a voice so happy I hardly recognized it.

I raced off without a backward glance at Ralph and

followed my mom and siblings to help. Ralph might be nice, but he wasn't my daddy.

I tossed and turned all that night with mixed feelings of anticipation and sadness, though they temporarily faded the next morning when we opened the presents piled high under the tree. Earlier, Mom had asked each of us what we'd like for Christmas. I asked only for a pair of ice skates (and secretly wished for my "real" father.) Although I opened several nice presents, there were no ice skates. Even that one little request seemed to go unanswered. Still, I knew I should be grateful. After all, my brother, sister, and I were finally reunited with our mother after a three-year separation.

"Well, let's gather up the wrappings and get some breakfast," said Mom.

"Good idea," Ralph agreed. "I'm hungry."

"Do you like your presents?" Ralph asked me as we all stood up.

"Yes," I said, trying not to show any disappointment.

"Well let's see what you have here," he said looking through my pile. "Oh my, Helen, something's wrong."

Mom took a closer look.

"Why, something is missing," she said. "I'm sure that Joanne has one more present."

The two of them grinned from ear to ear. Then I remembered how Mom had loved to play hide-and-seek games with us.

"You're getting warm . . . warmer. Now you're cold. Oh, you're really cold now."

My brother and sister excitedly raced around the house with me, trying to help, but I only grew more and more frustrated.

I stopped in the middle of the kitchen, feeling tense and angry. This was a dumb game.

Suddenly, Ralph's warm voice cut through my bitter thoughts. "Stop a minute. Think about where you've been."

My frustration quieted in response to his gentle voice, and I pondered my route. Recalling a "warm" message every time I got between the dining and living rooms, I stood under the archway in puzzlement. Dick must have been contemplating the route as well. He looked Ralph up and down and smiled. Dick looked at me, then up toward the ceiling. There on the archway shelf was a large decorated package.

Ralph, six feet, five inches tall, easily reached up and retrieved the box. Inside was a pair of bright, white ice skates. The ice skates were a beautiful gift, but the one I treasure most from that Christmas did not come wrapped in paper. It came in the package of a very tall police officer who loved our mother and us with all his heart. God knew best that Christmas for he brought me a very special dad to make us a whole family.

The Day My Faith
Meant Most to Me

GLENDA JONES

One afternoon in December, my little sister and I bounded off the school bus and into our house. Tonight would surely be different—tonight Mom would greet us with that special exuberant spirit all her own. The Christmas spirit was just too infectious, especially for Mom, who usually was the most susceptible one of all. Into the kitchen we trounced, bubbling over with joy. But the bubbles soon burst as we stared at the lone piece of paper lying on the table. My happy little world ended as I read Dad's familiar scrawl.

All we could see were those dreaded words looming before our eyes. "I have taken Mother to Cherokee . . . Dad." Cherokee was an accepted joke around our school.

Seldom did a day go by when someone didn't make some smart remark about a certain person being bound for a straitjacket at Cherokee. How I had howled at such humor then!

Never could I feel the same way again. It was as if a door of my life had slammed shut, denying me my former carefree days. Oh, I had known that Mom had not been alert for several months, but I had refused to face the situation. Now I had no choice but to accept the fact that Mom—my own mother—was mentally ill and might not be home for months!

And who did that leave in charge as "chief cook and bottle washer?" Me—fifteen-year-old me. Dazedly, I threw together a few meager scraps which hardly could be considered a meal. I was too stunned to care about anything except . . . what was I going to do? How could I manage a household and keep my grades up at the same time? Would I have to sacrifice my social life?

The back door slammed and my dad came in. Time can erase every other memory, but I can never forget his face at that moment—eyes so devoid of emotion and hope as to seem transparent, his whole face frozen in an expression of despair. One look and I knew that my problems were insignificant compared with those my dad had to shoulder.

Right then and there I made up my mind that, no matter what, our family would hold the fort for Dad's sake. Although I knew I could never replace Mom (and didn't intend to try), I would do my own best to make things easier for my family.

I could end the story right here by saying that turning to God in my hour of despair gave me the needed strength and confidence. But God was the farthest from my thoughts during that next week. After all, I reasoned bitterly, if God let such misfortune happen to a family who didn't deserve it, then surely my prayers—if even heard—would be unwelcome and go unanswered.

As if matters weren't already bad enough, gradually I began to feel sorry for myself—for the bad stroke of fate, for the additional responsibility and work. My temper became short. I would lash out at my little sister for leaving her dirty socks on the davenport. I would argue with Dad as though it were I who ran everything in the household. I couldn't understand the puzzled and hurt replies I received.

Finally December 24 arrived. But this year it was more than just Christmas Eve; it was the day at last that Dad and I could visit Mom. That morning, my bitter ways seemed sweetened somewhat by the magical effect of the day, and I began to think of someone beside myself. I began to realize what a lonely Christmas Mom and many others like her would be spending. By the time we were ready to leave, I was loaded down with presents—not only for Mom, but paper plates of candy and cookies my sister and I had made for others at Cherokee.

Since my dad had an appointment with Mom's doctor before we could visit her, I waited in the lobby. While sitting in the great hallway filled with other visitors and with patients going home for the holidays, my old resentment began to tug at my conscience. Once again I began to wonder how God could be so merciless as to let such an illness strike us.

"You look very sad," said a voice that snapped me back to reality. "That's no way to be on Christmas Eve." It was the elderly lady sitting next to me. In no time I was deep in conversation with her.

My new friend was of such a sunny nature that it came as a surprise for me to learn that her son was a patient in Cherokee. Later I learned that her daughter at home was paralyzed by polio from the waist down. Accepting her handicap, this girl had made the most of her abilities and was currently writing a novel. It seems impossible that with all the heartache she had suffered, this woman could be so cheerful and optimistic, so outgoing. Before I even realized it—I heard myself pouring out all my problems just as if she were an old friend.

When I had finished, she grew very serious and carefully explained to me how one simple act—prayer—had relieved her of an unaccountable amount of grief and had made her reliance upon God strong and vital. So at last was unlocked the mystery of this woman's cheerful perseverance. She soon made me realize that my prayers would have to be from the heart and not of a superficial type. When she had prayed for her children, she had asked God "to take care of them as He saw fit, not as I saw." In such a manner, must I ask God for help. For only then would I feel that my burden had been lightened. At last I realized that I had been shunning the only One who could help me but, nevertheless, He had been waiting patiently by my side until I could "see the light" and put my wholehearted trust in Him.

Maybe it was God watching over me who sent such a person to teach me one of the most important lessons of life. I'd rather believe that it was also the magic of Christmas Eve and the fact that on such a day, many years ago, the greatest miracle of all mankind took place, a miracle that made possible such minor miracles as had taken place this particular day.

Yes, the day my faith meant the most to me was the day I found it on a snowy Christmas Eve in the lobby of a mental hospital. There I found faith that sustained me over the year that my mother struggled up the rocky road to recovery.

The Christmas Miracle

SUSAN LEONARD

When I recall precious Christmas memories, I think of a very special story, one which represents the magic and glory of the season. This is a true story, as told to me by my husband—a professional Santa Claus—of a real Christmas miracle he experienced.

A few years ago, a little boy and his grandmother came to see my Santa at Mayfair Mall in Wisconsin. The child climbed up on his lap, holding a picture of a little girl. "Who is this?" asked Santa, smiling. "Your friend? Your sister?"

"Yes, Santa," he replied. "My sister, Sarah, who is very sick," he said sadly. Santa glanced over at the grandmother who was waiting nearby, and saw her dabbing her eyes with a tissue.

"She wanted to come with me to see you, oh, so very much, Santa!" the child exclaimed. "She misses you," he added softly.

Santa tried to be cheerful and encouraged a smile to the boy's face, asking him what he wanted Santa to bring him for Christmas. When they finished their visit, the grandmother came over to help the child off his lap, and started to say something to Santa, but hesitated. "What is it?" Santa asked warmly.

"Well, I know it's really too much to ask you, Santa, but . . ." the old woman began, shooing her grandson over to one of Santa's elves to collect the little gift which Santa gave all his young visitors. "The girl in the photograph . . . my granddaughter . . . well, you see . . . she has leukemia and isn't expected to make it even through the holidays," she said through tear-filled eyes. "Is there any way, Santa . . . any possible way . . . that you could come to see Sarah? That's all she's asked for, for Christmas, is to see Santa."

Santa blinked and swallowed hard and told the woman to leave information with his elves as to where Sarah was, and he would see what he could do.

Santa thought of little else the rest of that afternoon. He knew what he had to do. *What if it were my child lying in that hospital bed, dying,* he thought with a sinking heart. *A visit from Santa is the least I can do.*

When Santa finished visiting with all the boys and girls that evening, he retrieved from his helper the name of the hospital where Sarah was staying. He asked the assistant location manager how to get to Children's Hospital. "Why?" Rick asked, with a puzzled look on his face. Santa relayed to him the conversation with Sarah's grandmother earlier that day. "C'mon . . . I'll take you there," Rick said softly.

Rick drove them to the hospital and came inside with Santa. They found out which room Sarah was in. A pale Rick said he would wait out in the hall.

Santa quietly peeked into the room through the half-closed door and saw little Sarah on the bed. The room was filled with what appeared to be her family; there was the grandmother and the girl's brother he had met earlier that day. A woman whom he supposed was Sarah's mother stood by the bed, gently pushing Sarah's thin hair off her forehead. And another woman, who he discovered later was Sarah's aunt, sat in a chair near the bed with a weary, sad look on her face. They were talking quietly, and Santa could sense the warmth and closeness of the family and their love and concern for Sarah.

Taking a deep breath, and forcing a smile on his face, Santa entered the room, bellowing a hearty, "Ho, ho, ho!"

"Santa!" shrieked little Sarah weakly, as she tried to escape her bed to run to him, IV tubes intact. Santa rushed to her side and gave her a warm hug. A child the tender age of his own son—nine years old—gazed up at him with wonder and excitement. Her skin was pale and her short tresses bore telltale bald patches from the effects of chemotherapy. But all he saw when he looked at her was a pair of huge, blue eyes. His heart melted, and he had to force himself to choke back tears. Though his eyes were riveted upon Sarah's face, he could hear the gasps and quiet sobbing of the women in the room. As he and Sarah began talking, the family crept quietly to the bedside one by one, squeezing Santa's shoulder or his hand gratefully, whispering "thank you" as they gazed sincerely at him with shining eyes.

Santa and Sarah talked and talked, and she told him excitedly all the toys she wanted for Christmas, assuring him she'd been a very good girl that year. As their time together dwindled, Santa felt led in his spirit to pray for Sarah, and asked permission from the girl's mother. She nodded in agreement and the entire family circled around Sarah's bed, holding hands. Santa looked intensely at Sarah and asked her if she believed in angels. "Oh yes, Santa . . . I do!" she exclaimed.

"Well, I'm going to ask that angels watch over you," he said. Laying one hand on the child's head, Santa closed his eyes and prayed. He asked that God touch little Sarah and heal her body from this disease. He asked that angels minister to her, watch and keep her, and to give her family peace. And when he finished praying, still with eyes closed, he started singing softly, "Silent night, holy night . . . all is calm, all is bright." The family joined in singing, still holding hands, smiling at Sarah, and crying tears of hope, tears of joy for this moment, as Sarah beamed at them all.

When the song ended, Santa sat on the side of the bed again and held Sarah's frail, small hands in his own. "Now, Sarah," he said authoritatively, "you have a job to do, and that is to concentrate on getting well. I want you to have fun playing with your friends this summer, and I expect to see you at my house at Mayfair Mall this time next year!" He knew it was risky proclaiming that to this little girl who had terminal cancer, but he *had* to. He had to give her the greatest gift he could—not promises of dolls or games or toys—but the gift of *hope*.

"Yes, Santa!" Sarah exclaimed, her eyes bright. He leaned down and kissed her on the forehead and left the room.

Out in the hall, the minute Santa's eyes met Rick's a look passed between them, and the two men wept unashamed. Sarah's mother and grandmother slipped out of the room quickly and rushed to Santa's side to thank him. "My only child is the same age as Sarah," he explained quietly. "This is the least I could do." They nodded with understanding and hugged him.

One year later, Santa Mark was again back on the set in Milwaukee for his six-week seasonal job, which he so loved to do. Several weeks went by, and then one day a child came up to sit on his lap. "Hi, Santa! Remember me?"

"Of course, I do," Santa proclaimed (as he always does), smiling down at her. After all, the secret to being a good Santa is to always make each child feel as if they are the "only" child in the world at that moment.

"You came to see me in the hospital last year!"

Santa's jaw dropped. Tears immediately sprang into his eyes, and he grabbed this little miracle and held her to his chest. "Sarah!" he exclaimed. He scarcely recognized her, for her hair was long and silky and her cheeks were rosy—much different from the little girl he had visited just a year before. He looked over and saw Sarah's mother and grandmother in the sidelines smiling and waving and wiping their eyes.

That was the best Christmas ever for Santa Claus. He had witnessed—and had been blessed to be instrumental in bringing about—this miracle of hope. This precious little child was healed. Cancer-free. Alive and well. He silently looked up to heaven and humbly whispered, "Thank You, Father. 'Tis a very, merry Christmas!"

The Best Gift of All

MARY A. BOYD

My six-year-old son, Donald, had just started first grade at a local Christian school. My husband and I liked the teachers there and the fact that the small classes were made up largely of children from our church. Donald liked the school too.

One day Donald excitedly told me about a contest the school was going to have. It would be a "Math-a-Thon" to raise money for a children's hospital. The students would take a timed test and complete as many math problems as they could. Beforehand, parents and children would get pledges for every problem completed correctly. It was a school-wide contest, so the students would compete against children in all grades, from kindergarten through sixth grade. Donald could hardly wait.

The grand prize of the contest was a portable sterio with a tape player and big speakers. That stereo was the

coolest thing my son had ever seen, and he was determined to win it. He called all his relatives and neighbors
to get pledges, and he started working on sample math
sheets. Every day for several weeks he practiced taking
timed tests. I had never seen him work so diligently at
anything. His teacher was amazed because Donald would
even work on math sheets during his free time at school.
The other children and parents noticed his efforts too.

Then the big day arrived. After the tests were taken,
the entire school assembled in the chapel to hear the winner of the contest announced. Donald beamed when his
name was called as the grand-prize winner. Parents, teachers, and students all cheered. Everyone knew how much
this had meant to him. As soon as we got home, Donald
cleared a special place on his dresser for his new stereo.

Later that year Donald joined the Cub Scouts and was
in a den with several boys from his class. He worked hard
for his patches and learned the Scout motto about being
loyal and honest. As a service project, and to teach the
boys responsibility, one of the Scout leaders decided to
have the boys adopt an "angel," a child from the children's
home in our town. The boys would do odd jobs and save
money to buy this child a gift for Christmas. The Scout
leader explained to the boys that the children from this

home were less fortunate and the gift they gave their "angel" might be the only one he received for Christmas.

The child selected to be their "angel" was a nine-year-old named Roberto. The Scouts had two months to save money, and then they would go shopping for Roberto's gift. After the two-month period, all the boys met at our house and counted up the money they had saved. Despite their best intentions, they had only managed to come up with about twelve dollars. When they looked at Roberto's wish list, they saw that what he wanted most was a stereo, and twelve dollars was certainly not enough for one.

As the Scouts, their parents, and the Scout leader munched on snacks and talked about what to do for Roberto, I saw Donald go upstairs. After a few minutes, I saw him struggling to come down the stairs with a big box in his hands. He pulled the box into the room where all the boys and parents were eating and visiting. He just stood there silently until everyone turned and noticed him. He said that since they couldn't afford to buy a nice new stereo for Roberto, he wanted to give him the one he'd won in the contest.

For a few moments, no one spoke. Everyone in the room knew how much this stereo had meant to my son. I watched with tears in my eyes as the eight boys from his den gathered around Donald and helped him wrap his beloved stereo for Roberto. I expected Donald to cry, and I was already working out a plan to buy him another stereo, when I noticed the giant grin across his face. He was genuinely happy to be able to give this gift to Roberto. At only six years old, this little boy had shown us all the true meaning of Christmas. And, for me, that was the best gift of all.

A Gift to Each Other

KRISTI HEMINGWAY

I was born with a bit of a wandering spirit. After high school I went to college two states away, then joined a theater company and traveled all over North America and Europe. I was really far away and really broke most of the time, but no matter where I wandered, I made it home to Colorado for Christmas. This was a fairly significant feat, and yet I had managed to do it every year without fail. It sometimes involved days and nights of driving through blizzards, gallons of espresso, twelve-hour plane rides, connections that routed me in circles, lost baggage, and customs officials who always seemed to choose me to pick on.

Our holiday traditions were pretty average—tree, presents, way too much food, Christmas Eve service at church, watching the movie *White Christmas* with my sister. There was nothing extraordinary or even unique happening, but living so far away made it essential to be there. I needed to stay current in my siblings' lives. I wanted to know my nieces and nephews and have them know me. If I wasn't there for Christmas I feared I would just fade out of the family.

The year I got engaged, my fiancé, Calvin, and I traveled back to Colorado for the wedding. We were the "opening ceremonies" of a huge Fourth of July family reunion. We'd been doing an on-the-road version of dating for three years and figured, why wait? We threw the wedding into the mix since everyone would already be gathered. I wasn't a girl who imagined my wedding as the pivotal point of human history anyway; so a simple, thrown-together affair was just my style. But even small and simple broke the bank for us. We headed back to work in Europe knowing there would be slim chance of another trip home anytime soon. Christmas would likely be a cozy twosome.

"This is okay," I told myself, "We're our own family now. It will be romantic." Plus, our tour ended in Switzerland, so that's where we'd be stuck for Christmas. Definitely worse places to be! It would not be hard to make the best of this—a Christmas to remember!

But as the tour drew to a close, my morale crumbled.

Watching our teammates excitedly depart, talking about cherubic nieces and nephews, trees and stockings, and family traditions left me feeling less than lucky about my own situation. Yes, I was a newlywed and the world was supposed to be rosy, but in truth, spending our first six months of couplehood living out of a van with a team of kooky performers and sleeping on pull-out couches in people's dens had placed a strain on the marital bonding process. In fact, I really wouldn't recommend this plan to any sane person. Our harmony was a little off key, to put it mildly. Three solid weeks of undiluted togetherness was looking about as awkward as the sixth-grade dance and even less appealing. A little padding of friends and family would be so much less strenuous.

The lack of company wasn't the only check in my negative column either. We had no home. As I said, we traveled in a van and were housed as part of our performance contracts. Being on break meant that we'd have to find a place to stay. Someplace free. And who wants a couple of bickering vagabonds hanging around at Christmas? Even if someone did take pity and invite us into their "stable," I was really stretching to dig up any gratitude toward someone's pull-out couch.

Then there was the shortage of trappings and trim-

mings. Our performing-artist lifestyle left us without dis-
cretionary funds; so gifts were pretty much out. And to
top it all off, Calvin got sick with an infected wisdom
tooth. He was delirious with pain. So much for romance.
Elvis had pretty much nailed it. This was going to be one
"Blue-oo-ooo Christmas."

First things first. Although Calvin and I were alter-
nately ticked off and bewildered toward one another, I did
still have regular moments of fondness toward him. I didn't
enjoy seeing him in pain, especially because it made him all
whiny and meant I had to do all the driving. We needed to
get that tooth taken care of. We prayed.

"Lord, we haven't been very nice to each other lately,
and we know that bothers You. We're going to try and
improve, but in the meantime, Calvin's in a lot of pain and
it's Christmas and all, and we were hoping that maybe You
could toss us a miracle or something. A little sprinkle of
healing power. Please."

It was something like that. Not a very spiritual sound-
ing prayer, just desperate. Luckily, God seems to enjoy
those. We stopped on our way out of town at the home of
our area representative, Jean-Francois, to drop off a calendar for our next tour.

He took one look at Calvin and declared with

widened eyes, "*Zut Alors!*" This can mean many things, but in this case it was an expression of alarm.

He made a phone call. He spoke way too fast for me to follow his French, but it sounded very emphatic and convincing. Twenty minutes later the source of distress was being extracted from Calvin's jaw by Jean-Francois's personal friend, who also happened to be a dental surgeon and who also decided he didn't want to be paid since it was two days before Christmas. God is so cool, and His people can be really cool sometimes too. On this day He was also really speedy, which was such a nice bonus.

While Calvin was being repaired, I wandered the streets of Lausanne, soaking up Christmas spirit from all the colors and lights and using my tiny store of Swiss Francs to buy a few chocolate coins, a nice writing pen, a recording of Calvin's favorite artist, and a few other tidbits. I could wrap each one separately and tie little bows, and we could have a little miniature Christmas. It would be a peace offering—my promise of a fresh start. Our harmony had already improved with the pressure of the tour off our shoulders. A little privacy might be endurable after all.

With that thought came the reminder that we needed a place to stay. We had actually had an offer, but I was putting off phoning them. Timothy and Pierette are the elderly uncle and aunt of a colleague. They live in a remote mountain village a couple of hours from Geneva, and we had met them earlier that tour. Timothy is an egg farmer and Pierette runs the general store in the village. They mentioned that they had a "petite apartment" in their basement, and we were welcome to stay anytime. We told them we needed a place for the holidays, and they seemed thrilled at the thought.

Why hadn't I called them? I had a picture in my mind of a spider-infested stairway leading to a dank room with a bare flashlight hanging down, a chamber pot in one corner and a hot plate with questionable wiring in the other. I was thinking WWII French resistance. This would be the space between two walls where they hid Jewish neighbors and secret radios. Of course this was neutral Switzerland, so none of that actually happened here, but my imagination always tended toward the dramatic. There would be an old wooden door with a broken latch. Chickens would be pecking outside the door and snow would blow in through the cracks. We'd sleep on separate army cots under thread-bare blankets, and we'd have scrambled eggs for Christmas dinner. Truthfully, I was kind of reveling in the whole sad and wretched picture. My first Christmas away from home would become a classic Christmas tragedy like the *The Little*

Matchstick Girl or the *Gift of the Magi*. If they made a movie, maybe I could play myself.

I was brought back to reality when Calvin arrived, all swollen cheeked. "Tho, dith joo make dath phwone cawwl?"

We really had no alternatives, but I was sure the expe-rience itself wouldn't be as fun or glamorous as the eventual movie version. I tried to find solidarity in my heart with the Virgin Mary and the whole stable experience. I assured myself I would grow spiritually through this, but that wasn't very comforting—about as soothing as the last week of my telling Calvin how much better he'd feel just as soon as we could somehow get that excruciating, throbbing tooth yanked out of his head. Not helpful.

I prayed again. "God, I miss my family. So far, marriage is not really the fun and games I expected, and I feel like Heidi going to stay on some mountainside in a scary basement with some old people I don't really know. I want to make the best of this. I know it's really not all about me. I know I should ask You to help me grow up and be selfless like You, but I want to pray that we have a really nice, fun holiday together. I don't suppose I could ask for both?"

I made the call, got directions, and turned the van up

the winding mountain road. It was hard to remain stoic with Calvin finally out of pain and dazzling snow smoothing over sharp edges and erasing every smudge with glowing whiteness. It was the afternoon of Christmas Eve as we headed for the village of La Cote Aux Fees, hoping not to miss it, as the entire village was apparently only about two blocks long.

We pulled into town early afternoon and had to wait for a herd of cows making its way down "main street" ahead of us. With Calvin mumbling the directions through wads of cotton we arrived in front of a three-level catawampus building with a big *Amueblements* sign hanging across the front. That's French for "this 'n' that." This must be Pierette's general store.

"Here goes," I sighed, forcing a resigned smile. Calvin returned a lopsided but cheerful smile. He was high on painkillers. What did he know?

I knocked hesitantly. The door flew open and Timothy and Pierette greeted us like their own long-lost grandchildren back from a war, or a refugee camp, or from just having received a Nobel Prize. We were ushered directly into the parlor where the scene drew us in like a warm bed on a cold night. A fire was crackling, a tree twinkling. There were needlepoint seat covers, a crocheted tea cozy, and china cups with tiny rosebuds on them. There were cookies right out of the oven and hot chocolate with lots of whipped cream.

Over steaming cups they asked us all about our tour, all about our wedding, all about our families. We learned all about egg farming and life in a tiny Swiss village. We laughed and smiled and ate cookies until I'd lost all track of time. God had answered my prayer before I even prayed it. He knew what I needed. He knew what our marriage needed, and He prepared this place for us long in advance. This was the most calm, nurturing place in the world to spend Christmas, or any other day for that matter. Of course I hadn't seen the "petite apartment" in the basement yet, but Pierette said we were welcome to join them upstairs as much as we liked, so maybe we wouldn't have to hang out with the spiders.

The phone rang, piercing the relaxed pleasant tones of our conversation. We heard a "*Zut Alors!*" in the conversation. This time it was alarm mixed with you've got to be kidding me. Timothy returned to us with a frown.

The village was in an uproar. The pastor was sick. He had a fever and had lost his voice. There would be no one to do the Christmas Eve program. This was a considerable crisis. This was tantamount to the breakout of the plague or a foreign army marching over the Alps. Timothy and Pierette exchanged distressed glances, and Pierette immediately began clearing away the dishes. Whenever a solution is unclear, it's always helpful to tidy up.

Calvin and I were experiencing a very different set of emotions and glances. He raised an eyebrow at me, and I answered with a grin and a nod. This was a no-brainer! We jumped up, offering in enthusiastic French unison, "We'll do it!"

We'd been doing nothing but Christmas programs for weeks. We had a vast repertoire to choose from. There was a frozen moment where Timothy's brain clicked. We could hear it. Then the dawning relief spread over both their faces and they breathed out a happy, "*Mais bien sur!*" But of course!

We immediately began gathering props, running lines, and planning all the music we could do with only the two of us. With a quick change of clothes we set off. We chose a play about two lonely people who meet in an airport on Christmas Eve. As the characters hesitantly and somewhat suspiciously began to converse, they share their stories, their loneliness, and a reminder of God's gift to us in the birth of Jesus. My character, a believer, realizes that they were put there for that reason—put there to answer one another's need. They read the Christmas story from the book of Matthew, and shared an impromptu celebration.

Calvin's character, with spiritual eyes opening for the first time, declares, "You'll have to lead me. I've never had a real Christmas before."

We were in the zone. We were a perfect team that night, and, like a tidal wave washing over me, I remembered why I had chosen to spend the rest of my life with this man. Performing this play on Christmas Eve for these people was perfect. There was laughter and sniffles and spontaneous expressions of emotion. As I spoke my lines, the truth of them penetrated my own heart—we answered each other's need. We were put here for that reason. Don't you see it? The paradox of God's sovereignty struck me. Somehow, in the complexity of God's love and provision, it is all about me. He cares about my smallest details and desires. And yet, at the same time, it's all about Calvin, and it's all about the man in the front row with tears streaming down his cheeks, and it's about Pierette and her general store, and the dental surgeon, and each of my teammates at home with their families. We are God's gift to each other. Like a master composer, He brings all the instruments together, each with a different tone, each playing a different part, and He makes it turn out so beautiful.

After the program we were invited to the evening meal, full of cheese and chocolate and all the yummiest things from Switzerland. Not a single scrambled egg. We loved hearing about these people's lives, so different from our own. We walked up the main street, back toward the *Amueblements*, marveling at how bright the stars are in the mountains. We grabbed our suitcases and at last made it down the staircase to the place that would be home for the next three weeks.

The staircase was steep, and the basement was indeed dark and creepy. We opened the door and were greeted by twinkling lights, a small decorated tree in the corner, and evergreen boughs, all adorning a newly remodeled, sparkling clean studio apartment. There was modern plumbing and a real stove and refrigerator with perfect wiring. There was a tantalizing fruit basket on the table and a big, soft bed covered with the whitest and fluffiest down comforter I'd ever seen. Calvin spontaneously lifted me over the threshold.

"Merry Christmas," I sighed. He set me down, wrapping his arms around me. I wrapped back. We were God's gift to each other. This was where I was meant to be.